MANCHESTER UNITED LEGENDS

Written by Adrian Besley

sona BOOKS

© Danann Media Publishing Limited 2023

First published in the UK by Sona Books, an imprint of Danann Media Publishing Limited 2023

WARNING: For private domestic use only, any unauthorised Copying, hiring, lending or public performance of this book is illegal.

CAT NO: SONO563

Photography courtesy of

Getty images:

Matthew Ashton	Clive Brunskill	Julian Finney
Laurence Griffiths	Adrian Dennis / AFP	Michael Regan
Bryn Lennon	Stringer	Lluis Gene
Matthew Peters	Wesley	Mark Leech / Offside
Paul Popper / Popperfoto	Maja Hitij	Phil Cole
Tom Purslow	Mark Thompson	W & H Talbot Archive
John Peters	Christian Liewig / Corbis	Alexander Hassenstein
Hulton Archive	Manchester United	Richard Heathcote
Mirrorpix	Shaun Botterill	Lee / Stringer
Dan Mullan	Alex Livesey	Professional Sport
Bob Thomas	NurPhoto	Ross Kinnaird
Ash Donelon	Paul Ellis	Andrew Yates
David Cannon	Joe Klamar	

All other images, The Press Association, Wiki Commons

Book cover design Darren Grice at Ctrl-d

Layout design Alex Young at Cre81ve

Copy Editor Martin Corteel

Proofreader Finn O'Neill

All rights reserved. No Part of this title may be reproduced or transmitted in any material form (including photocopying or storing it in any medium by electronic means and whether or not transiently or incidentally to some other use of this publication) without the written permission of the copyright owner, except in accordance with the provisions of the Copyright, Designs and Patents Act 1988. Applications for the copyright owner's written permission should be addressed to the publisher.

Every effort has been made to acknowledge correctly and contact the source and/or copyright holder of each picture and Sona Books apologises for any unintentional errors or omissions, which will be corrected in future editions of the book.

Made in EU.

ISBN: 978-1-915343-28-4

CONTENTS

INTRODUCTION	8
UNITED LEGENDS	10
GEORGE BEST	12
SIR BOBBY CHARLTON	20
ERIC CANTONA	28
DUNCAN EDWARDS	36
RYAN GIGGS	42
DENIS LAW	50
PAUL SCHOLES	58
MARCUS RASHFORD	66
WAYNE ROONEY	74
CRISTIANO RONALDO	82
TOP 50 GREATEST PLAYERS OF ALL TIME	90
TOP 5 GREATEST MANAGERS OF ALL TIME	106
ERNEST MANGNALL	108
SIR MATT BUSBY	110
TOMMY DOCHERTY	112
RON ATKINSON	114
SIR ALEX FERGUSON	116
TOP 10 GREATEST TEAMS OF ALL TIME	118
TOP 10 GREATEST GAMES OF ALL TIME	130

INTRODUCTION

Manchester United are the biggest club in the world. In match attendances, global fanbase, trophies won, star players and commercial value and revenue, the Red Devils are peerless. They have won 12 FA Cup finals, been champions of England 20 times, champions of Europe three times and have even taken home the FIFA Club World Cup. Their history sparkles with passion, panache, glory and, of course, the greatest of tragedies.

Around the globe the club is known for playing football in the right way — stylish, attacking and always entertaining. In the following pages we feature the players, managers and teams who have created this

stature and reputation, recalling their immense talent and character, as well as their greatest achievements.

Manchester United's rich tradition is built on the club's legends; the players who have led or starred in those great sides. This book spotlights the contributions of the prolific goalscorers, from Stan Pearson to Marcus Rashford; the inspirational captains, from Martin Buchan to Steve Bruce; the goalkeepers, from Peter Schmeichel to David de Gea; and the club heroes who bleed red and white, like Ryan Giggs, Gary Neville, Nobby Stiles and Paddy Crerand. It focuses on the superstars who have graced Old Trafford and taken United to stratospheric levels. Crowd favourites such as Wayne Rooney and Denis Law, heroes like Bobby Charlton and Paul Scholes, the shooting star that was Duncan Edwards, and the pure genius of Eric Cantona and George Best.

The architects of those great teams have not been forgotten either. Compared to most clubs, in their long history Manchester United have had surprisingly few managers. Matt Busby and Alex Ferguson kept the seat for 50 years between them, each developing super-talented players and producing not just one, but several iconic teams. Then there are Ernest Mangnall, Tommy Docherty and Ron Atkinson, who all played their part in building United's reputation and adding silverware to the trophy cabinet.

The Red Devils' greatest and never-to-be-forgotten players, matches, teams and managers are drawn together here in a celebration of the club's glittering and exhilarating history. These are the legends of Manchester United.

▼ View of The Sir Alex Ferguson Stand (North Stand) seen from the Sir Bobby Charlton Stand (South Stand) at Old Trafford

UNITED LEGENDS

Here are the ten greatest Manchester United players of all time — the true legends. No doubt you can predict who some of the players are, but others may surprise you. Are they all strikers? Which midfielders have made it? Are there any defenders on the list or could a goalkeeper have slipped in? Even if you're prepared to go along with the names, do you agree with the rankings? Read on to find out!

▶ Fans celebrating Sir Alex Ferguson during the Barclays Premier League match against Swansea City on 12 May 2013 – his last home game in charge after announcing his retirement. The banner also pays tribute to fan favourite and playing legend Paul Scholes who had retired for the second time

GEORGE BEST

TWO-FOOTED, PACEY AND WITH PERFECT BALANCE

He was the first real footballing celebrity, known as much for his behaviour off the pitch as on it, so it's easy to forget what an extraordinarily talented footballer George Best was. However, that talent undoubtedly makes him worthy of the number one spot in the list of Manchester United legends.

▶ George Best, 15 April 1968

▼ Best with Northern Ireland in 1976

470 APPEARANCES
179 GOALS

GEORGE BEST

13

George Best was born in Belfast, in Northern Ireland, in 1946. He was a bright boy and at the age of 11 he passed the 11-plus exam and went to a high school that played rugby union. However, he quickly switched to a secondary school specialising in football, because that was where his interests and indeed his abilities lay. He played as a winger and was already exhibiting an impressive natural facility with the ball.

When he was 15, he was spotted by a Manchester United scout, who famously sent a telegram to manager Matt Busby, telling him he'd discovered a genius. That scout wasn't wrong. After a trial, Best was signed by United and moved to Manchester, but was terribly homesick and only stayed two days. He came back, though, and spent a couple of years as an apprentice (in fact, officially he had amateur status as English clubs couldn't employ Northern Irish apprentices at that time), signing professional papers on his 17th birthday in May 1963.

That year, Best made his debut for United, the club

PORTUGAL'S MEDIA DUBBED BEST 'O QUINTO BEATLE' — THE FIFTH BEATLE

◄ Matt Busby shares his joy and the European Cup with Pat Crerand and George Best, 30 May 1968

► Focus on George Best magazine feature

with which he is most associated and the club where he spent most of his playing career, on 14 September in a 1-0 win against West Bromwich Albion. He didn't make the first team again until 28 December, when he managed to get his name onto the scoresheet in a 5-1 victory over Burnley. Busby continued to pick him and by the end of the 1963-64 season he had scored six goals in 26 appearances. The team finished second to Liverpool in the league and went out of the FA Cup to West Ham in the semi-finals stage, although Best did captain the side that won the 1964 FA Youth Cup — the first time United had won that particular tournament since the Munich air disaster of 1958.

Best's first full season as a regular in the first team was 1964-65, when he made 59 appearances and scored 14 goals. Along with Bobby Charlton and Denis Law — the three of them are immortalised in the United Trinity statue outside Old Trafford — he was instrumental in United winning Division One for the first time since Munich. Their principal rivals were Don Revie's Leeds United, heading for their most successful era, and the race for the title came down to goal average, but it was clinched by a 1-0 United victory at Elland Road. The Whites did, however, knock the Red Devils out of the FA Cup in the semi-finals.

The game that clinched superstardom for Best, though, was the following season's European Cup quarter-final against Benfica at the Estádio da Luz in Lisbon on 9 March 1966. He dismantled the Portuguese team almost single-handedly and scored two of the goals in United's 5-1 win. His dark, shaggy mop-top hair led Portugal's media to dub in *O Quinto Beatle* — the Fifth Beatle.

However, United went out of the European Cup in the next round, to Belgrade's Partizan, in mid-April. Best played, but his knee was strapped up, injured after a game against Preston North End in late March.

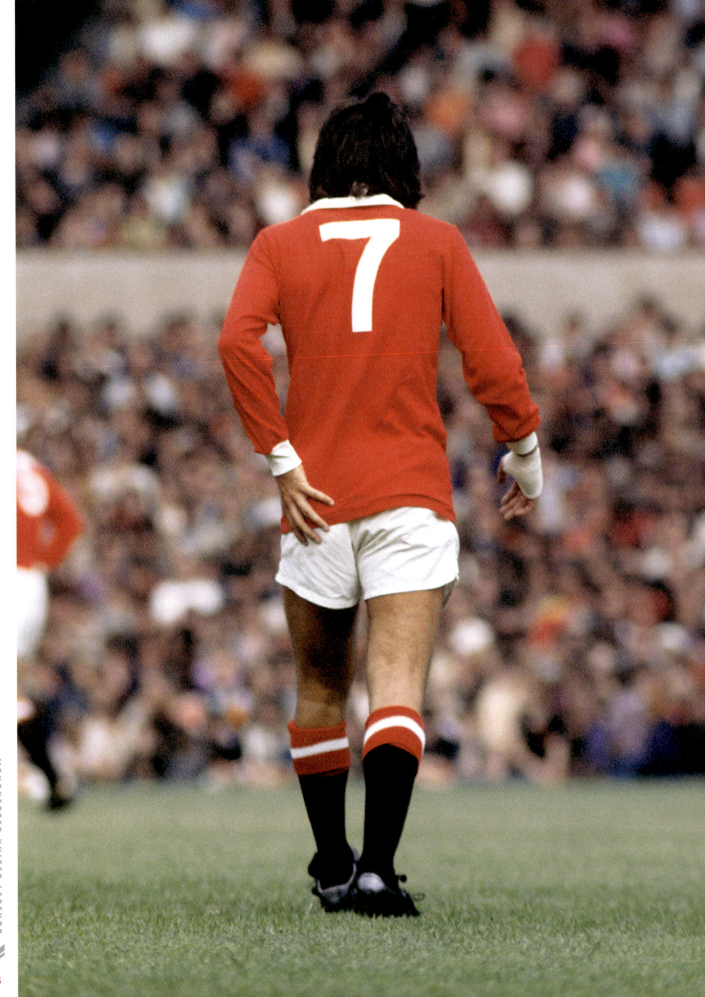

> **BEST COULD CREATE CHANCES OUT OF NOWHERE AND THEN CONVERT THEM**

The club finished fourth in the league and reached the semi-finals of the FA Cup, not the final, so 1965-66 had been, on balance, good for Best himself, but was a season without honours for Manchester United.

When the following season, 1966-67, drew to a close, though, Manchester United had won the First Division title with apparent ease, four points ahead of Nottingham Forest and Tottenham Hotspur, who both finished in second place (Forest had the slightly better goal average). Best had been a constant in the team, playing 45 times and scoring 10 goals.

In the season after that, Manchester United frustratingly lost the title to rivals Manchester City by a mere two points, but United fans chiefly remember the 1967-68 season because their team won the European Cup, exactly ten years after the Munich air disaster. Even though by this time European teams were wise to Best's abilities and attempted to neutralise him, he was still integral to that victory.

Having beaten Hibernians from Malta, United got the better of the Yugoslavian team Sarajevo 2-1, with Best scoring one and assisting on the other. In the quarter-finals they disposed of Polish club Górnik Zabrze 2-1 to face Real Madrid in the semi-finals. The only goal of the home leg — a superb 15-metre strike — was scored by Best and in the away leg, despite being marked very tightly, he got in a crucial cross to Bill Foulkes, who found the back of the net. That game ended 3-3 and United went through 4-3 on aggregate. In the final against Benfica at Wembley, it was 1-1 at full-time, but Best scored the vital goal after two minutes of extra time and it finished 4-1 to United.

That year, Best was joint top-scorer in the First Division (with Ron Davies of Southampton). He was also presented with the Football Writers' Association Footballer of the Year award and the European Footballer of the Year award (then known as the Ballon

▲ Best leaps for the ball – Manchester United v Leeds United, FA Cup semi-final at Villa Park, 3 January 1971

◀ Classic shot of George Best, 18 September 1971

d'Or), ahead of Yugoslavia's Dragan Džajić, Germany's Franz Beckenbauer and his own teammate, Bobby Charlton. He was still only 22.

Best stayed at United for another six years, until 1974, but that year of 1968 was the pinnacle of his career and, for a while, United's fortunes, too. Matt Busby retired in 1969 and there were several years that were devoid of success — by United's standards at any rate — including relegation to Division Two in 1973-74.

▼ Best arrives in Rotterdam, the Netherlands, October 1976

▶ Man City v Man United, Mike Summerbee of Manchester City, George Best and Bobby Charlton, 6 November 1971

He began to pick up regular bookings, would get sent off, failed to make it to a match he was scheduled to play in, missed training — on at least one occasion for a whole week — usually to go partying and clubbing. He fell out so badly with Bobby Charlton that he refused to play in Charlton's 1972 testimonial. On the other hand, though, he was capable of getting hat-tricks or going on an extended run and beating a series of defenders before scoring a breath-taking goal.

At the end of 1971-72 he announced his retirement, but then turned up for pre-season training and continued to play. During 1972-73, when Tommy Docherty was made the new United manager, he announced his retirement again, but then continued to play again. His final game for the club was on 1 January 1974, away to Queens Park Rangers, but it was a low note to go out on as they lost 3-0.

As a boy, Best was skinny and slight, and when he first arrived at United, Busby made sure that training sessions were sometimes tough, so that Best learned to cope with rough challenges designed to counteract technical prowess. Two-footed, pacey and with perfect balance, Best could create chances out of nowhere and then convert them. Able to control the ball with exquisite precision, he was the master of the feint and could dribble past defenders with ease. He enjoyed outwitting those opponents, not just with his skills, but with clever tricks, and he understood that football is not only about winning, it's also about entertaining.

In 470 appearances for Manchester United over 11 years George Best scored 179 goals and was frequently the club's top scorer of the season, plus he won those two league titles, the 1968 European Cup and was named European Footballer of the Year in 1968. He is also the post-war record-holder for the most goals scored by a United player in one game, having

put six past Northampton Town in a 1970 FA Cup fifth-round game that finished 8-2.

As well as being Manchester United's greatest ever player, Best was almost certainly Northern Ireland's. He had 37 caps between 1964 and 1977 and, although he never played in a World Cup, he said he really enjoyed international football, because, playing for a smaller country like Northern Ireland, the pressures were far less than they were when he played for his club.

It's all too easy to theorise about Best's decline. Perhaps the money, even though it was far less than players earn today, was too much, because it enabled him to have the extravagant and flamboyant lifestyle he could seem to handle. Perhaps the attention and the pressure of being in the spotlight was too much. Perhaps even if he hadn't become an iconic footballer he would have developed the personal problems, most significantly alcoholism, which were well-publicised and which plagued him for the rest of his life.

In the ten or so years after he left United, Best played for clubs in Scotland, Ireland, the United States, South Africa and Australia, as well as Fulham, Bournemouth and Stockport County, but often for extremely brief periods of time, although he did manage over 50 appearances for both the Los Angeles Aztecs and the San Jose Earthquakes in the States.

After he retired from football, he occasionally appeared as a pundit, but his money and health issues continued. In 2002 he had a liver transplant and in 2005 he died, at the age of 59, due to complications arising from the immunosuppressive drugs he had to take as a result of the transplant.

SIR BOBBY CHARLTON

KNOWN FOR HIS FIERCE LONG-RANGE SHOT AND HIS STAMINA

Sir Bobby Charlton's legendary status derives in part from his England career and his membership of the team that won the World Cup in 1966, but he played almost all his club football in Manchester and his passion and commitment to United truly embodied the values of the club.

◀ Charlton takes a corner in front of an expectant crowd

▶ Bobby Charlton, 26 August 1969

Bobby Charlton was born in the mining town of Ashington, Northumberland in 1937. His father was a miner, but there were several footballers in the family on his mother's side — four of his uncles played professionally and his mother's cousin was Newcastle United and England legend, Jackie Milburn. Of course, his older brother, Jack, became a footballer, too, for Leeds United, so perhaps it's fair to say that football really was in his blood.

At any rate, he was spotted by a Manchester United scout while playing for East Northumberland schools, and signed as an amateur with United in 1953, when he was 15, and turned professional in 1954. He played for the youth team and then the reserves, scoring frequently, before making his first-team debut at 18, on 6 October 1956, against Charlton Athletic, a match that the Reds won 4-2.

However, he was simultaneously doing his National Service in Shrewsbury with the Royal Army Ordnance Corps. Between 1950 and 1960 young British men were obliged to spend two years serving in the armed forces and Matt Busby had suggested he applied to that particular part of the army, because he would be able to continue playing for United at the weekends. He was in Shrewsbury at the same time as his equally talented teammate Duncan Edwards.

In his initial first-team season Charlton played 14 times and scored 12 goals, including two on his debut and a hat-trick in the return Charlton Athletic match, which the Reds won 5-1 as they progressed towards and eventually took the 1956-57 First Division title. They faced Aston Villa in the 1957 FA Cup Final, so there was a chance of the Double, but unfortunately the game was marred by controversy.

Just six minutes after kick-off, Villa centre-forward Peter McParland and United keeper Ray Wood clashed. Wood, unconscious and with a broken cheekbone, had to be stretchered off. However, this was in the days before substitutes were permitted and it looked like Charlton would be called upon to go in goal, but in the event it was Jackie Blanchflower who drew the short straw. Wood eventually came back on and stood

> **IN HIS INITIAL FIRST-TEAM SEASON CHARLTON PLAYED 14 TIMES AND SCORED 12 GOALS**

◀ Bobby Charlton (centre) lines up with his teammates the day before the Munich air disaster, 8 February 1958

▶ Bobby Charlton, sitting up in his bed in Munich Hospital

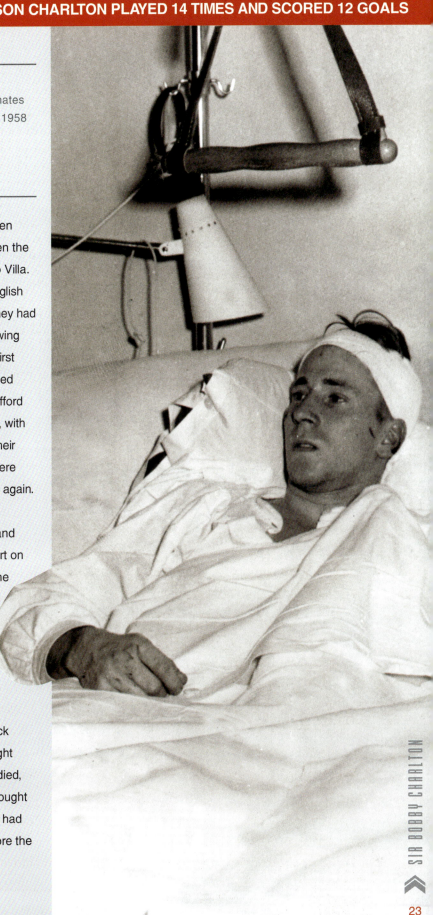

around, before going back in goal for the last seven minutes. Blanchflower had done very well between the sticks, but conceded a couple and it ended 2-1 to Villa.

In 1956-57 United had also become the first English team to compete in the European Cup, although they had lost in the semi-finals to Real Madrid, and the following season, with Charlton now well-established in the first team and one of the Busby Babes, they had qualified again. They beat Red Star Belgrade 2-1 at Old Trafford in the first leg of the quarter-finals and were 3-0 up, with Charlton contributing a brace, in the second leg. Their opponents managed to level it to 3-3, but United were ahead on aggregate and through to the semi-finals again.

On that fateful day of 6 February 1958 Bobby Charlton was on the plane that failed to take-off and crashed at the end of the runway at Munich airport on the journey back to Manchester. He was one of the lucky ones, though, pulled from the wreckage by goalkeeper Harry Gregg, who thought he and teammate Dennis Viollet were dead, but dragged them away from the aircraft anyway, before going back to rescue Matt Busby and Jackie Blanchflower.

Charlton had minor head injuries, severe shock and spent a week in hospital, but he survived. Eight of the side were among the 23 passengers who died, including Tommy Taylor and David Pegg, who thought sitting at the back of the plane would be safer, so had swapped seats with Charlton and Viollet just before the attempted take-off.

NAMED FOOTBALLER OF THE YEAR BY THE FOOTBALL WRITERS' ASSOCIATION

Bobby Charlton was still only 20 years old. The tragedy made a massive impact on him — how could it not? — and it has been said that every game Charlton subsequently played, he played for those teammates who passed away as a result of Munich air disaster. He must surely have still been traumatised, and Busby himself was still recovering from his significant injuries, but Charlton re-entered the fray swiftly. His first game back was on 1 March and it was an FA Cup quarter-final match against West Bromwich Albion. It was a 2-2 draw, but United went through on the replay, 1-0.

Unsurprisingly, United started to drop points in the league and eventually finished in ninth position. They also went out of the European Cup at the semi-finals stage, losing 5-2 on aggregate to AC Milan, who were themselves beaten 3-2 by Real Madrid in the final. In terms of salvaging United's season, that left the FA Cup and miraculously they had dispensed with Fulham after another replay and made it through to the final, where they met Bolton Wanderers. The day of the final coincided with Matt Busby returning to work after the air crash and it would have been some sort of fairy-tale ending if the Reds had lifted the trophy, but sadly Nat Lofthouse hit the back of the net twice and victory was Bolton's.

Obviously the team had to be rebuilt and there were five years when United didn't win any sort of trophy, but Charlton was at the heart of the side that eventually tasted success again by beating Leicester City 3-1 to lift the 1963 FA Cup trophy. League championship wins in 1965 and 1967 followed, although for Charlton personally the intervening year, 1966, was memorable, as not only was he a World Cup winner, but he was named Footballer of the Year by the Football Writers' Association and made European Footballer of the Year (at that time called the Ballon d'Or) as well. He was runner-up for the latter in 1967 and 1968 too.

However, surely the highlight of Charlton's career with the Reds was when he captained the team that, exactly a decade after the tragedy of the Munich air disaster, won the 1968 European Cup. What's more, on an emotional evening at Wembley, he scored twice as Manchester United beat Benfica 4-1 after extra time and became the first English club to win the tournament. When he lifted that trophy no doubt he was thinking of those who were not there, but should have been.

◀ Charlton on the cover of Argentinian sports magazine *El Gráfico*, 27 June 1962

▶ 1968 European Cup Final programme

It was soon back down to earth with a bump, though, as the early 1970s were not filled with glory for Manchester United and the trio of Charlton, Best and Law fell out, which didn't foster stellar on-field performances. Charlton left the club at the end of 1972-73 — personal relations were so poor that Best refused to play in his testimonial — so he missed relegation to the second division at the end of the next season.

What was remarkable about Bobby Charlton was his ability to send a pass through from midfield, his fierce long-range shot and his stamina — he was never a player who would give up. He was also versatile in terms of where he could play. At various times he took on the roles of central-midfielder and left-winger, but it was perhaps as an attacking midfielder that he was most effective. His final goal for Manchester United was away to Southampton on 31 March 1973, when the Reds won 2-0, with his final game for the club a month later, on 28 April 1973, away to Chelsea, although on that occasion the Reds lost 1-0.

It was the end of an era, one that had lasted 17 years. Charlton held the record for appearances in a red shirt — 758 — for 35 years until Ryan Giggs overtook him in 2008. He held the record for goals scored in a red shirt — 249 — for almost 45 years until Wayne Rooney overtook him in 2017. If there was any doubt about his stature at Manchester United, he is depicted standing with George Best, beside Denis Law, in the United Trinity statue at Old Trafford.

Of course, this was also alongside his international career. He was in the squad for four World Cups and played in three, winning the trophy with England in 1966, and when he retired from the national team in 1970 he had 106 caps, making him the most capped player ever (Bobby Moore overtook him in 1973), and had 49 goals to his name (Wayne Rooney — again — overtook him in 2015).

After he left Manchester United, Charlton became manager and then player-manager at Preston North End, and was briefly caretaker manager at Wigan Athletic. He played a few games in Ireland, Australia and South Africa, pursed his business interests and appeared as a pundit on the BBC. He was always a great ambassador for the game and, following in the footsteps of Matt Busby, in 1984 he became a director of Manchester United and, again like his former mentor, he was knighted in 1994, having already received an OBE and a CBE. He stood down from the club's board in the late 2010s and in 2020, when he was 83, it was announced that he had received a diagnosis of dementia.

◀ Captain Bobby Charlton (centre) with Nobby Stiles (left) and veteran Bill Foulkes (right) on a lap of honour after Manchester United beat Benfica of Portugal 4-1 at Wembley to win the European Cup, 29 May 1968

▼ Bobby Charlton takes on the Spurs defence, White Hart Lane, 3 February 1968

ERIC CANTONA

POWER MIXED WITH SKILL, CREATIVITY AND AN ABILITY TO SCORE

Compared to some of the other greats who have graced the hallowed turf of Old Trafford, King Eric's reign in a red shirt was relatively short. He ruled supreme for a mere four and a half seasons, but his impact was immense and he is undoubtedly Manchester United royalty.

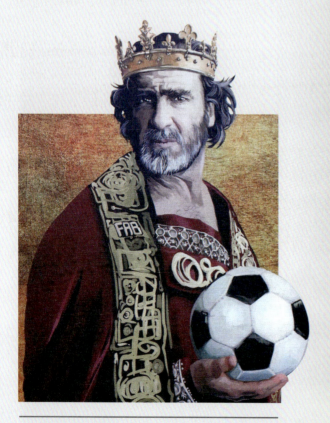

▲ King Eric - footballing royalty

◀ Eric Cantona celebrates during an FA Premier League match against Manchester City at Old Trafford, United won the game 2-0 with both goals scored by Cantona, 23 April 1993

182 APPEARANCES
82 GOALS

Frenchman Eric Cantona, born 1966, played a crucial role in Manchester United's dominance in the 1990s, but when he arrived at the club in November 1992 he was 26, an experienced footballer and a veteran of not just six French clubs, but also, controversially, Leeds United. In fact, with his trademark turned up collar, Cantona proved to be no stranger to controversy during his time at Manchester United.

Prior to Cantona's arrival, United's season had not really caught fire. They were trailing in the race to win the first Premier League title and had found goals hard to come by. However, Cantona, who made his debut as a sub at home to Manchester City on 6 December — United won 2-1 — quickly fitted in upfront beside Mark Hughes, while Brian McClair was moved to midfield.

A week later and he bagged his first goal for the club against Chelsea at Stamford Bridge — the result was 1-1. His second was in another draw, this time 3-3, against Sheffield Wednesday at Hillsborough on Boxing Day, but he didn't just get his own name on the

> **CANTONA WAS ALLOTTED 7, A NUMBER WHICH WAS ALREADY ICONIC**

◄ Cantona shields the ball from Brian Gayle of Sheffield United during a Premiership match at Old Trafford in 1993

► Eric's iconic collar up, chest out pose

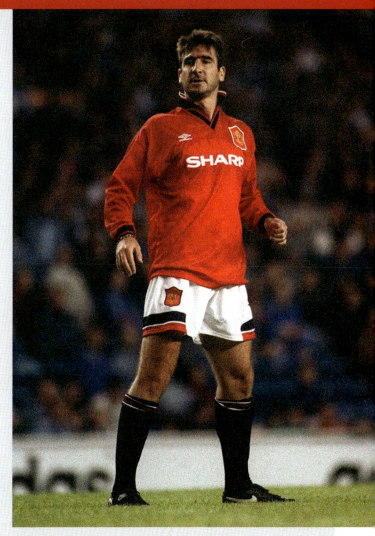

scoresheet, he was also adept at creating chances for other players, too.

It wasn't long, though, before controversy reared its head and his disciplinary card was marked. In February, back at Elland Road to play Leeds, he was on the receiving end of torrents of abuse from home fans and retaliated by spitting at one of them. The match was a 0-0 draw and Cantona was given a £1,000 fine by the FA.

After Cantona joined United they only lost two league games that season and finished it as the first champions of the Premier League era, ten points clear of nearest rivals Aston Villa. It was fair to say that in a matter of a few short months the volatile Frenchman had made his presence felt!

United were on a high and that continued through to 1993-94, because not only did they win the Premier League title for a second consecutive season — their nearest rivals, Blackburn Rovers, finished eight points behind them — but they also achieved the Double by beating Chelsea in the 1994 FA Cup Final. The first two goals, both of which were penalties, came from Cantona and helped secure the 4-0 win.

In 1993-94, personal squad numbers on shirts were introduced, rather than numbers based on the position a player was playing in. Cantona was allotted 7, a number which was already iconic, having been worn by both Bryan Robson and George Best, and which he retained for the rest of his time at United (the Champions League system was different and his number was usually 9). That season Cantona was also the club's top scorer, with 24 goals in total, and was named the Professional Footballers' Association Player of the Year.

However, he also had his disciplinary struggles. In the autumn of 1993 he was sent off against Galatasaray as United went out of the Champions League in the second round. In March 1994 he was also sent off, twice this time, in consecutive league games against Swindon Town and then Arsenal, meaning a five-match ban, which covered an FA Cup semi-final against Oldham Athletic. That game was a 1-1 draw, but fortunately Cantona could play in the replay and with his participation the Reds won 4-1, progressing to the final and eventually that Double.

THE FRENCHMAN'S RESPONSE WAS TO LAUNCH A KUNG-FU-STYLE KICK

United's objective for 1994-95 was obviously a third consecutive league title and ideally another Double, and for the first half of the season everything seemed on track for that. Blackburn led the league, but the Reds put them under a lot of pressure, not least by winning 4-2 away at Ewood Park on 23 October, a game in which Cantona scored. He also scored on 10 November, in a 5-0 trouncing of Manchester City, and then on 22 January he got the only goal when Blackburn made the return visit to Old Trafford.

At that point he had 12 league goals plus one from an FA Cup third round victory against Sheffield United. However, three days after the Blackburn game, on 25 January 1995, an incident during a game away to Crystal Palace put a stop to Cantona's goal tally and, ultimately, United's bid for a third successive Premier League title.

Throughout the game Cantona had been marked very tightly by Palace defender Richard Shaw. Eventually he kicked out at Shaw, which resulted in a red card. As he trudged towards the tunnel, Cantona encountered a Palace fan called Matthew Simmons, who shouted abuse at him. The Frenchman's response was to launch a kung-fu-style kick at Simmons, followed by several punches.

The fracas made international headlines and it was obvious Cantona would receive a ban, but the question was for how long? Under FA instructions, Manchester United fined Cantona £20,000 and banned him from playing for the first team for the rest of the season, but the FA then fined him an additional £10,000 and increased the ban to eight months. He also lost the French national side's captain's armband and, in fact, never played for France again.

However, on top of all this, he was charged with assault. When he appeared in court on 23 March he pleaded guilty and was given a two-week prison sentence, but was freed on bail pending an appeal. The appeal court overturned the sentence two weeks later and instead he received 120 hours of community service as punishment. He served this by coaching children.

Cantona's season was over and in reality so was United's. Granted, the club still managed second place in the league to Blackburn and were runners-up to Everton in the FA Cup — more than worthy achievements for anyone else, but not for United. There was nothing for it, but to regroup and go again.

Speculation was rife that once the suspension was over Cantona would head off to play abroad, but, deeply frustrated — he couldn't even play in friendlies — at the start of the 1995-96 season he went as far as to hand in his notice, saying that he didn't want to play football in England any more. However, Ferguson refused to accept his resignation and persuaded him to stay. Cantona later acknowledged that fans consider the attack against Simmons to be an iconic moment, but that from his perspective it was a deeply regretted mistake.

His first game after serving the ban was on 1 October 1995 at home to Liverpool. After just two minutes he set up Nicky Butt to score and then, after Ryan Giggs was fouled, he put away a penalty himself. Cantona looked like he was most emphatically back, but in fact having been out for eight months he struggled to find his form right up until the new year.

◀ Cantona walks off after receiving a red card for kicking out at Palace defender Richard Shaw. A steward attempts to calm Palace fan Matthew Simmons in vain, the abusive comments he aimed at Cantona would result in the Frenchman landing a flying kick on the fan and landing himself in court

Come mid-January, though, United went on a run of 12 games without being beaten and Cantona was at the heart of a winning streak that included his return to Selhurst Park, where Wimbledon were ground-sharing with Crystal Palace. Cantona scored twice as United beat Wimbledon 4-2.

On 20 March, Cantona hit a stunning 25-metre half-volley, the only goal of the game against Arsenal, which meant that United overtook Newcastle at the top of the table. That game was the third in a run of six consecutive league games in which Cantona scored. Then in the last but one game of the 1995-96 season he got the fifth in a 5-0 win over Nottingham Forest and all the Reds had to do was not lose to Middlesbrough on the last day of the season. In they event they won 3-0 to claim their third league title in four years, with Cantona the club's top scorer on 14.

To cap it all, they met Liverpool in the FA Cup Final, with Cantona taking the captain's armband in place of the injured Steve Bruce. Cantona also volleyed in the only goal of the game four minutes from the end of normal time. United had not just won the FA Cup, they had won the Double again — the first team to do it twice!

A dominant physical presence on the pitch, Cantona combined his power with skill, creativity and an ability to score. He was versatile, too, able to take on the role of classic striker, traditional centre-forward or deep-lying forward, as well as attacking midfielder. He was always an intelligent playmaker, but elegant with it and a real joy to watch.

United retained the league title in 1996-97 and, due to the departure of Steve Bruce, Cantona retained the captaincy, but at the end of the season he unexpectedly announced his retirement from football, at the age of 30. His last competitive fixture was against West Ham on 11 May 1997, a game the Reds won 2-0.

With Manchester United alone, Cantona won four Premier League titles and two Doubles, and scored 82 goals in 182 appearances. He subsequently pursued a career as a theatre and screen actor, and won the 2005 FIFA Beach Soccer World Cup as player-manager of the French national side.

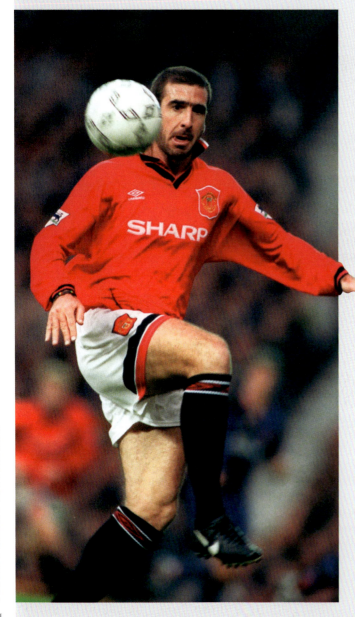

◀ Cantona in action during the FA Premiership match between Manchester United and Middlesbrough at Old Trafford, October 1995

▶ Alex Ferguson congratulates his captain Eric Cantona after United's 1-0 victory over Liverpool in the 1996 FA Cup Final at Wembley, 11 May 1996

DUNCAN EDWARDS

KNOWN FOR HIS TOUGHNESS, COMMANDING ON-FIELD PRESENCE

He was the archetypal Busby Babe and a footballing prodigy. Precious little footage of him exists, but those who saw him play often described him as a footballing genius. Tragically, Duncan Edwards was just 21 when he died of injuries sustained in the Munich air disaster, but he left an indelible mark on Manchester United.

◀ Football trading card – Duncan Edwards

▶ Duncan Edwards training, August 1954

177 APPEARANCES
21 GOALS

> **HE QUICKLY BECAME A FIRST-TEAM CHOICE, PROUDLY WEARING THE NUMBER 5**

◀ Sixteen-year-old Duncan Edwards sprints off the pitch after taking part in his first senior game, 4 April 1953

Duncan Edwards was born in Dudley, in the West Midlands, in 1936, and played football for his school and various other teams, including Dudley Schools, and Birmingham and District. He also represented his school as a morris dancer and was chosen to compete at the National Morris and Sword Dancing Festival. However, the English Schools Football Association also offered him a trial for the Under 14s, but unfortunately the trial was on the same day as the festival. He had to make a choice between dancing and football — and he chose football.

With his performances for England Schoolboys, Edwards attracted attention from several First Division sides, but in 1952 it was United he signed for. He initially played in the youth team, the team which went on to win the first ever FA Youth Cup, but by that time he had already made his first-team debut against Cardiff City. That was in April 1953 and United lost 4-1, but Edwards was 16 years and 185 days old, making him at that point the youngest player ever to play English league football. He quickly became a frequent first-team choice, proudly wearing the number 5 shirt.

Along with the likes of Jackie Blanchflower, Bobbie Charlton, Bill Foulkes, Wilf McGuinness (who subsequently managed the club himself) and Dennis Viollet, Edwards was one of the young players brought in and developed under the auspices of manager Matt Busby from the late 1940s through the 1950s, to replace the older players in the squad who were nearing retirement. As a group, these youngsters were known as the Busby Babes.

In the 1953-54 season Edwards made 24 appearances in the league, plus he was in the team when United went out of the FA Cup early on to Burnley, although he still turned out regularly for the youth squad as well and played in the team that won the Youth Cup for the second consecutive time.

In 1954-55 he played for the first team 36 times, establishing himself as the first-choice left-half. He also scored six senior goals, but he was still eligible for the youth team, so played in the club's third successful Youth Cup Final as well. (It's safe to say that Manchester United dominated this competition until the late 1950s.)

More or less the only blot on Edwards' copybook during his time at United — and in terms of the way some of today's footballers behave it seems incredibly mild — was that he couldn't drive and would cycle to and from Old Trafford on his Raleigh bike. One evening, he was cycling home after the team had lost when a policemen stopped him for not having any lights on his bike. The Magistrates Court fined him 10 shillings (50p in today's money) and the club docked him an additional two weeks' wages for bringing the club into disrepute.

United won the league in both 1955-56 and 1956-57, with Edwards playing in, respectively, 33 and 34 games in each season, and taking his total number of appearances for the club to over a 100. He was part of the team that lost the 1957 FA Cup final to Aston Villa, losing the Double in the process, and he also participated in United's first ever European Cup campaign, in which they reached the semi-finals, where they were knocked out by Real Madrid.

The 1957-58 season dawned and as well as chasing a third consecutive league title and kicking off their FA Cup campaign, United were in competition for the European Cup again. In the preliminary round United beat Shamrock Rovers 9-2 over two legs. In the first proper round they took on Dukla Prague and beat them 3-1 on aggregate. That put them through to the quarter-finals, where they were to meet Red Star Belgrade.

> **MANY OF HIS FELLOW PROFESSIONALS HAVE SAID HE WAS AMONG THE GREATEST**

The first leg was at Old Trafford on 14 January 1958, which United won 2-1. The return leg was in Belgrade on 5 February. That was a 3-3 draw, but it was sufficient to put United through into the semi-finals 5-4 on aggregate.

Because they'd experienced hold-ups coming back from the previous leg in Prague, the club had chartered its own plane to fly the players, staff and journalists home. The take-off was delayed for an hour because Johnny Berry, who at 31 was the oldest in the team, had mislaid his passport and once it did get going it had to stop in Munich to refuel.

However, it was snowing heavily and two attempts to take off again had to be abandoned. The pilot decided to make a third attempt, but the aircraft wasn't going fast enough for flight — it was later determined slush slowed the plane down — and it ran out of runway, crashing into a house and a hut, which was filled with fuel that exploded.

Twenty people, including seven players, three staff and two journalists died at the scene of the crash. Two players, Johnny Berry and Jackie Blanchflower, were so badly hurt that they never played again and Matt Busby himself was so seriously injured that he had to spend two months in hospital and was twice given the last rites.

Duncan Edwards survived the crash, but was also very badly injured, with fractured legs, broken ribs and kidney damage. Although it seemed unlikely he would play again, his friends believed he would pull through, because he was physically strong and a real fighter, but 15 days later, on 21 February, he tragically died.

The final death toll of the Munich air disaster was 23, as Frank Swift, another journalist and a former goalkeeper who had played with Busby, had died en route to the hospital and co-pilot Ken Rayment also died in hospital.

Hugely popular with fans, Edwards was a defensive midfielder known for his toughness, commanding on-field presence and the way he took control on the pitch. He would implacably stonewall an attacking player from the other team, only to pick up the ball from them, dance round them and head for goal.

Many of his fellow professionals have said he was among the greatest — if not the greatest — they had played with and against. Of course he had his faults — he was still so young and his game was still developing — but he spent less than five years with United and who knows what heights he might have conquered with the club if he had had the chance.

◀ The plane wreckage in the snow, Munich air disaster, 6 February 1958

▶ Football trading card – Duncan Edwards

RYAN GIGGS

A MASTER OF CHANGING THE PACE AND LAUNCHING ATTACKS

The best Manchester United player of the modern era? Some would say so. Over 23 years Ryan Giggs made 963 appearances for Manchester United, largely on the left in midfield, and he scored 168 goals. He is the archetypal one-club man — except he started his footballing career with Manchester City.

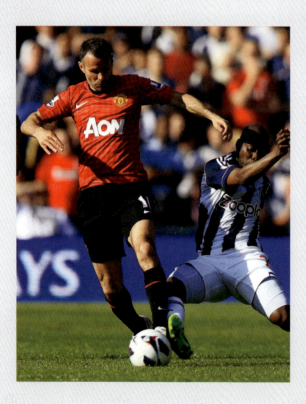

◀ Ryan Giggs takes on Youssuf Mulumbu of West Brom during their Barclays Premier League match at The Hawthorns, 19 May 2013

963 APPEARANCES
168 GOALS

◀ Ryan Giggs in Premier League action against West Brom at The Hawthorns, 19 May 2013

Ryan Giggs was born in Cardiff in 1973, moving to Salford as a six-year-old, when his father, who was a professional rugby player, joined local rugby league side Swinton RLFC (now known as Swinton Lions). Giggs also played rugby league at schoolboy level, but as a youngster he showed great ability with the round ball as well and so joined the local football club, Deans. They were coached by a scout for City and he recommended Giggs to City, who signed him up to their School of Excellence. Meanwhile, he moved on to play for Salford Boys.

However, having seen Giggs play for Deans, an Old Trafford steward spoke directly to Alex Ferguson about the lad and Ferguson sent a scout out to watch him. The long and the short of it was that, as a result, on the boy's 14th birthday, Alex Ferguson turned up at Giggs' family home and offered him a two-year schoolboy contract with the promise that he could turn professional in three years, when he was 17. Needless to say, the young Giggs grabbed the chance with both hands.

Just as Ferguson had promised, Giggs made his professional debut for the Reds in 1991, when on 2

> **NEEDLESS TO SAY, THE YOUNG GIGGS GRABBED THE CHANCE WITH BOTH HANDS**

◀ Ryan Giggs takes on Michael Tarnat and Oliver Kahn in the Champions League 1998-99 Final against Bayern Munich, Barcelona, 26 May 1999

March he came on as a sub, for Denis Irwin, against Everton. This was in a First Division match, before the launch of the Premier League. He made his first proper start in the league later that season, on 4 May, in a game against City and even — this is the stuff of dreams — managed to get on the scoresheet, although admittedly his winning goal did take a substantial deflection off Colin Hendry.

At that point Alex Ferguson hadn't been at United that many years and his long winning streak was just beginning to get going. More to the point, though, he had been searching for a reliable left-sided player for a while — and it looked like he had found one in Giggs.

In the November of the following season, 1991-92, United triumphed in the European Super Cup final against Red Star Belgrade and Giggs picked up his first senior medal. In the April he picked up his second when the Reds beat Nottingham Forest to win the League Cup. That season his peers voted Giggs PFA Young Player of the Year and they did the same again the next year, making him the first player in history to receive the award in two consecutive years.

In such a lengthy and consistent career as Giggs had there were many, many highlights, but winning the very first Premier League title in 1992-93 must surely be one of his most memorable moments. He was also a crucial part of the Double-winning sides of 1993-94 and 1995-96, and then the Treble-winning side of 1998-99. He made his mark on that Treble-winning campaign with an extraordinary FA Cup semi-final solo goal against Arsenal. That strike, which won goal of the season and is generally considered to be one of the greatest ever goals scored by a Manchester United player, sent the Red Devils through to ultimately win the FA Cup component of the Treble.

Although testimonials are usually held at the end of a career, on 2 August 2001 Giggs's first ten years of service in a red shirt were commemorated with a testimonial against Celtic at Old Trafford. In front of a crowd of 67,000 (which is what the capacity of the stadium was back then) United lost 4-3, but nonetheless it was a clear sign of the esteem in which Giggs, who wasn't quite 28, was held by the fans and the club itself. Just over a year later, on 23 August 2002, he notched up his 100th career goal, away to Chelsea, in a game that ended 2-2.

Fast-forward to 2007, which turned out to be a year full of personal milestones for Giggs. In May, when, after three years of second and third place, United won the league title, he picked up his ninth league champions' medal and overtook Liverpool stalwarts Alan Hansen and Phil Neal who had eight apiece.

In June, so that he could concentrate on prolonging his club career, he stood down from international football, having played 64 games and scored 12 goals for Wales. In October, his contract with Manchester United was extended to June 2009, when he would be 36, although in the event he went on playing for another five years after that. In December, he scored the opener and his 100th league goal in a game that saw United beat Derby County 4-1 at Old Trafford. Also in December, he was awarded an OBE for services to football.

On the footballing front, the 2007-08 season was Giggs's 18th with United's first team. He captained the side on many occasions, but especially so in 2007-08, when Gary Neville, who usually pulled on the armband, was frequently beset by injury.

▶ Giggs and Evra pose with the trophy after beating Chelsea on penalties in the final of the UEFA Champions League at the Luzhniki stadium in Moscow, 21 May 2008

GIGGS CONTINUED TO CONTRIBUTE OUTSTANDING PERFORMANCES

The last league game of that season was away to Wigan Athletic on 11 May 2008. United's goal difference was excellent, but in order to secure the title they had to do as well as or better than Chelsea, who were playing Bolton Wanderers. The Wigan game was also Giggs's 758th in a red shirt, which meant he had equalled Bobby Charlton's record, and Giggs also scored the second goal, which made the scoreline 2-0 to United and, with the Chelsea game a draw, comfortably sealed that second title in a row for the club.

United's season wasn't over, though, and on 21 May 2008 they faced Chelsea at the Luzhniki Stadium in Moscow in the final of the Champions League. The game was 1-1 after extra time, so it went to penalties. After six attempts, both sides had missed one and Giggs, who had come on as a sub towards the end of the second half, stepped up to take the seventh shot for United. He scored and, when Edwin van der Sar saved Nicolas Anelka's kick for Chelsea, that proved to be the decider — Manchester United had won their third Champions League trophy.

▼ Giggs lifts the trophy as Manchester United celebrate after a victory over Chelsea in the final of the Champions League 2008

2009, 18 years after he had won the junior version, he was made PFA Player of the Year. That showed what his fellow professionals thought of him and then, on 30 November 2009, which also happened to be his 36th birthday, he was named BBC Sports Personality of the Year, which was a mark of how well-regarded he was by the general public.

He may not have been quite so fast as he once was and he was increasingly used as an impact sub, but his footballing brain was a sharp as ever and in the last five or so years of his playing career Giggs continued to contribute outstanding performances for Manchester United, although in 2012-13, when Alex Ferguson finally retired, he had to adjust to playing under a new manager, David Moyes, for the first time in

Towards the end of the 2013-14 season, after David Moyes had been sacked, Giggs was announced as interim player-manager and then, after four games in charge, he was named as assistant manager to Moyes's replacement, Louis van Gaal. This was on 19 May 2014 — the same day that he officially retired as a player (that year, along with several teammates from the Class of '92, he also took at 10% stake in Salford City FC).

In July 2016, after José Mourinho had been appointed to replace Van Gaal, Ryan Giggs left Manchester United after over two decades. His name was linked to various clubs, but in January 2018 Giggs became the manager of the Welsh national side, for whom he had made 64 on-field appearances, and under his guidance Wales qualified for the 2020 Euros.

However, because of the Covid-19 pandemic the tournament was delayed until 2021 and by the time it took place Giggs had stood down as manager. This was due to issues in his private life and an impending court case in which he was charged with assault. The jury in that case failed to reach a verdict and at the time of writing the case is set to be retried in summer 2023.

Those 963 appearances give him the club's record for appearances — he overtook Bobby Charlton when the team beat Chelsea in Moscow to secure the 2008 Champions League. And that longevity of service is part of the reason why he is the player who has won most honours with the club. He has 13 Premier League winners' medals, which is more than any other player at any other team. He has also won four FA Cups, three League Cups and two Champions Leagues, plus nine Community Shields, a Club World Cup, a Super Cup and an Intercontinental Cup.

Ryan Giggs had exceptional control and could cross a ball with precision. He could read a game perfectly, knowing exactly when to hold the ball up, launch an attack or change the pace. He was indisputably one of the greatest — if not the greatest — players of his generation.

▼ The Manchester United team line up with the Champions League trophy after their dramatic win, 26 May 1999

DENIS LAW

HE WAS DETERMINED IN HIS PURSUIT OF GOALS

As a mark of his importance to the club, Denis Law features in the United Trinity statue in front of Old Trafford along with George Best and Bobby Charlton. However, he is also the subject of a statue at the Stretford End, making him the only player to have two stadium statues dedicated to him.

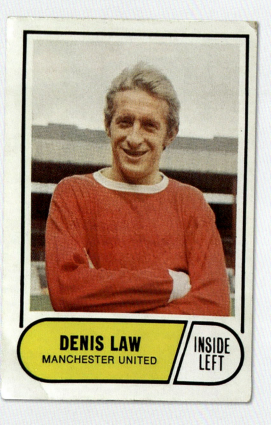

◀ Football card 1969-70 – Denis Law inside-left

▶ Denis Law in action

404 APPEARANCES
237 GOALS

DENIS LAW

Denis Law was a real flair player who scored 237 times in 404 appearances during his 11 years at Manchester United (only Bobby Charlton and Wayne Rooney have scored more). Born in 1940 in Aberdeen, he was the youngest of seven and his family certainly wasn't wealthy. It's said he didn't own a pair of shoes, let alone a pair of football boots, until he was 12 and even then they were hand-me-downs. As a lad he was football mad and rejected a place at the local rugby-playing grammar school so that he could attend a secondary school where they played football.

Having started off as a full-back, he moved to inside-left and played for Scotland Schoolboys. However, at 15 he was spotted by legendary manager Bill Shankly and, now playing centre-forward, signed for Division Two side Huddersfield Town. Law had been born with a squint and, although it didn't seem to affect his performance on the pitch unduly, Shankly arranged for him to have surgery to correct it.

Law spent four years at Huddersfield, before moving, at 20, to Manchester City for what was then a record British transfer fee of £53,000. Just over a year later he

> **HAVING SCORED 30 GOALS IN 37 GAMES, LAW'S CONTRIBUTION WAS DECISIVE**

◄ Denis Law (centre) celebrates with Maurice Setters and David Herd with the trophy after beating Leicester in the 1963 FA Cup at Wembley, 25 May 1963

► Denis Law in action, 10 September 1966

was on the move again, to Turin, this time for a record fee for a transfer involving a British player of £110,000. He had a successful season in Italy and learnt a lot, but wanted to come back to the UK — and Matt Busby wanted to bring him back to the UK, which is what he did, for yet another record transfer fee, of £115,000.

Law flew back to Manchester, boarding with the same landlady with whom he had stayed when he was playing for City, and made his debut for United against West Bromwich Albion on 18 August 1962, scoring first in a 2-2 draw. In terms of the league it wasn't a stellar season, as the team finished 19th, but Law was top scorer on 29 goals and also got the opener in the FA Cup Final against Leicester, which United won 3-1.

That was just the warm-up, though. The following year, 1963-64, the team did go out of the FA Cup at the semi-final stage, having lost 3-1 to West Ham, but they finished second in the league, with Law top scorer again, although this time he scored 46 in 42 appearances across all competitions, a club record that stands to this day.

However, the 1964-65 season was really the one that established him as a United legend. This was the season in which the team won the First Division championship for the first time since the 1958 Munich air disaster. It was a close-run thing, though, as they lost the last game of the campaign to Aston Villa. That meant they finished level on points with Leeds United and it all came down to goal difference.

Having scored 30 goals in 37 games, Law's contribution was the decisive factor that tipped the balance in favour of the team in red. That also led to him being named 1964 European Footballer of the Year — an enormous mark of respect for any player, but Law is also the only Scottish player to have been honoured in that way.

UNITED WON ANOTHER FIRST DIVISION TITLE IN 1967 AND LAW WAS TOP SCORER

Law was clearly immensely valuable to the club and, perhaps conscious that being a professional footballer was a very short-lived career, in 1966 he dared to ask Matt Busby for a pay rise, saying he would leave if he didn't get one. Busby responded by immediately putting Law on the transfer list, insisting no player would get away with holding the club to ransom. When a contrite Law went to see him, he produced a written apology and made Law sign it before showing it to the press. Law later insisted Busby had actually given him the pay rise, but in secret because he didn't want other players following suit. Either way, the upshot was Law stayed at United.

United won another First Division title in 1967 and Law was top scorer again, but unfortunately, laid low by injury, he wasn't in the side that won the 1968 European Cup. While his teammates, including his close friend George Best, who had been a first-team regular since the 1964-65 season, were busy beating the Portuguese side and two-time winners Benfica 4-1 in the final, Law was laid up in a hospital in Manchester, recovering from an operation on his right knee (he had missed the semi-final second leg against Real Madrid, too).

He had originally picked up the injury while on duty for Scotland in 1965 and it troubled him throughout his career. He would need regular cortisone injections to help the pain, but training and playing while still carrying the injury inevitably caused long-term damage. In January 1968 a specialist had advised that a previous operation to remove some cartilage hadn't worked and recommended a second operation.

◀ Denis Law of Manchester United in action in 1972

Law had continued playing almost until the end of the season, when the operation became unavoidable. The day after the final, though, he had a visit from Matt Busby himself, who could no doubt imagine what it must feel like to miss out on such a great occasion, and he brought the European Cup trophy along with him to show Law.

Winning the European Cup was an amazing achievement and, unsurprisingly, United failed to repeat the feat the following year, although, despite going out in the semi-finals to AC Milan, Law still managed to be the tournament's top scorer with nine goals.

In fact, the team struggled to attain the same level of success for a while and went through an uncharacteristically fallow period for a few years. Busby retired and was succeeded by Wilf McGuinness, Frank O'Farrell and then Tommy Docherty, who was apparently recommended to the board by Law, who knew him from playing with the Scottish national team.

Best and Charlton, the other two elements of the so-called Holy Trinity, had already left the club and after over a decade of service it was time for Law to depart, too. In July 1973 he was given a free transfer. He didn't want to leave the Manchester area as his family were settled there, so he rejoined Manchester City.

He spent just the one season there, but at the end of that season, in a derby match against his former club United, he scored in the 81st minute to make it 1-0 to City. In fact, United were technically already relegated, but Law's infamous back-heeled shot undoubtedly exacerbated the humiliation. He was devastated and immediately asked to be substituted. When asked about it in later years, Law confessed he had seldom felt as terrible as he did after scoring that goal.

▼ Denis Law (left) with his Manchester United teammates as Matt Busby holds the First Division championship trophy aloft to the applause of his players, 13 May 1967

Having first been capped as an 18-year-old, Law made a total of 55 appearances for Scotland and holds the Scottish international record for number of goals scored — 30 — jointly with Kenny Dalglish. He retired from football after the 1974 World Cup in West Germany, where Scotland held Brazil to a 0-0 draw and remained unbeaten, but went out at the first group stage on goal difference.

Denis Law was an immense talent, but not, perhaps, your typical centre-forward. Indeed, some have described him as a proponent of total football before the term had been invented. Not content to let others be the playmaker, he would get involved in every aspect of the game, tackling, taking on the role of a creative midfielder, dodging defenders — a skill he honed in Italy — or turn defender himself.

Predictably, United fans nicknamed him the Lawman, but, more appreciatively, they also called him the King. He was determined in his pursuit of goals and could chip the keeper, blast it, score from a tap-in or a

header, and he certainly wasn't averse to a back-heel or a bicycle kick.

Fans of opposing clubs, on the other hand, called him Denis the Menace, because he was often mischievous and it could be quite frustrating to find yourself up against him. It was the days before elaborate celebrations became the norm, but when he scored he would run, his arm raised, his finger pointing to the sky, yet it was an expression of joy rather than arrogance.

That tenacity and eye for a goal sometimes meant he was hauled up sharply by referees. He put this down to the fallout from an incident in 1962, when he and Matt Busby had reported referee Gilbert Pullin to the FA for taunting Law during a game against West Bromwich Albion. Pullin was heavily criticised by the FA and gave up refereeing as a result, but Law always felt this had turned him into a "marked man" in the eyes of match officials. Who knows whether that's true or not, but Law wasn't above arguing with a ref and he did have a fairly lengthy disciplinary record, particularly for a forward.

He went on to have a career as a TV pundit and he did a lot of charity work, including setting up the Denis Law Legacy Trust, but in 2021, when he was 81, he announced that he was suffering from a combination of Alzheimer's disease and vascular dementia.

PAUL SCHOLES

KNOWN FOR HIS LATE, ATTACKING RUNS AND HIS LINK PLAY

In his playing days, Paul Scholes was the archetypal "creative midfielder", comfortable in attack or defence, and happy to move out wide or take on the role of playmaker. He was also an archetypal "one-club man", who spent his entire career in a red shirt, playing for Manchester United.

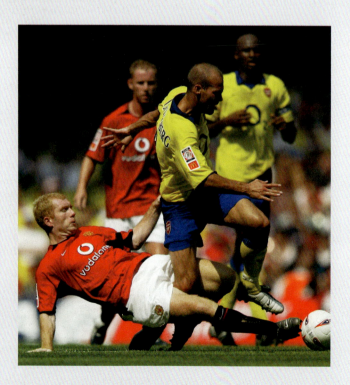

◀ Paul Scholes tackles Freddie Ljungberg of Arsenal during the FA Community Shield match, 10 August 2003

◀ Paul Scholes applauds fans after being substituted during his own Testimonial match against New York Cosmos at Old Trafford, 5 August 2011

718 APPEARANCES
155 GOALS

▲ Paul Scholes receives the Manchester United Young Player of the Year award, 3 May 1993

Like a number of his famous teammates, Paul Scholes emerged from the Manchester United Academy during Alex Ferguson's reign as manager. A local lad, he was born in Salford, in Greater Manchester, in 1974, grew up in Langley, also in Greater Manchester, and as well as showing great promise as a footballer, he was also a very good cricketer. He trained with United from the age of 14, signed on formally as a trainee at 17 in 1991 and turned professional in 1993.

Although he was part of the youth team that reached the FA Youth Cup final in 1992-93, he didn't make his first-team debut until a couple of seasons later, against Port Vale, in a September 1994 League Cup match in which he scored two goals, the final scoreline being 2-1 to United. His first league game came shortly afterwards, away to Ipswich Town, and although on that occasion United lost, 3-1, Scholes did manage to get himself on the scoresheet.

In early December, when the Reds travelled to Loftus Road where they beat Queens Park Rangers 3-2, Scholes netted twice. Then in early January he got the opener in a 2-0 victory at home to Coventry City — the first time he'd scored at Old Trafford — and Coventry were the opponents again when he scored in a 3-2 away win at the start of May. In all, during the 1994-95 season he made 17 league appearances and scored five goals, which wasn't bad for the new boy. He also came on as a sub in the 1995 FA Cup Final and almost scored twice late in the game, but in the end United lost to Everton 1-0.

In June 1995, Mark Hughes's second stint at United ended and he moved to Chelsea, and as the 1995-96 season began Eric Cantona was still suspended as a result of the assault on a Crystal Palace fan,

> **SCHOLES WAS INTEGRAL TO THE TEAM'S VICTORIES IN ALL THREE COMPETITIONS**

so Scholes was given more opportunities to play for the first team and for the first couple of months he partnered Andrew Cole up front. This was the season United became the first team to win the Double for a second time and Scholes's tally was 14 goals in all competitions.

As preparations for the next campaign began, Ferguson, on a quest for a new striker, was keen to sign Alan Shearer, but apparently Blackburn Rovers wouldn't contemplate a deal unless Scholes went to Blackburn as part of it. Obviously the transfer didn't happen, but it was a nice compliment for Scholes and even without the future *Match of the Day* pundit United achieved another Premier League title. Having originally been allocated shirt number 24, Scholes was now given shirt number 18, which he kept until he retired.

By United's high standards, 1997-98 was an unsuccessful season and although they came close, finishing second in the league and exiting the Champions League at the quarter-finals stage, it ended trophyless. That was followed, though, by new pinnacles of achievement as United won the Treble and Paul Scholes was integral to the team's victories in all three competitions.

▼ Manchester United players celebrate their second goal by Scholes in the 1999 FA Cup Final against Newcastle United at Wembley Stadium

SCHOLES NOTCHED UP 20 GOALS IN ALL COMPETITIONS — A CAREER HIGH

A constant in the league, he was also responsible for one of the two goals conceded by Newcastle United in the 1999 FA Cup Final. In the Champions League he scored an important away goal against Inter Milan in the quarter-finals and appeared as a substitute in the semi-finals away leg against Juventus, although unfortunately a yellow card incurred in the match meant he wasn't eligible to play in the final, against Bayern Munich, which Manchester United won 2-1.

As the 1999-2000 season and a new millennium dawned, the Reds were bidding once again for the Premier League title and in March Scholes scored one of his most majestic — if not the most majestic — goals, when, from just outside the box he volleyed David Beckham's corner kick superbly, sending it smartly over Dwight Yorke's head and curling it into the corner of the Bradford City net. Yorke had already got two, so it was 3-0 and Beckham subsequently made it a decisive 4-0.

Scholes followed up a week later with the first hat-trick of his professional career. United's opponents were West Ham and United's 7-1 win put them a whole ten points clear at the top of the table. They were still top at the end of May. (This was the season when United didn't take part in the FA Cup, because they entered the Club World Championship in Brazil instead.)

They took the league title again in 2000-01, but slipped to third in 2001-02, behind Arsenal and Liverpool, going out of the FA Cup in the fourth round. The Argentinian Juan Sebastián Verón arrived at Old Trafford at the start of that season and Ferguson, in order to make the most of all the talents at his disposal, stuck doggedly to a 4-4-1-1 formation, playing Verón and Roy Keane in central midfield with Scholes tucked in behind Ruud van Nistelrooy as a "withdrawn striker".

It was business as usual, though, in 2002-03 as they were victorious in the league again, with Scholes notching up 20 goals in all competitions — a career high watermark — including a hat-trick against Newcastle in a 6-2 win. He continued to both make and score goals. In 2003-04 the Reds finished in third place in the league once more, but Scholes got the winner against Arsenal in the semi-final of the FA Cup, putting them through to the final against Millwall, which they won 3-0.

The year after that was something of a repeat performance as not only were they third again, but they made the FA Cup final again too. This time, however, they lost to Arsenal after it had gone to penalties and Scholes's shot was saved by Jens Lehmann.

By now Scholes was over 30 years of age and in the second half of the following campaign he had to stop playing due to persistent blurred vision. There was talk that this could be the end of his career, but he recovered sufficiently to make an appearance in the last game of the season, against Charlton Athletic, and was fit again for the next season, marking 500 games in a Manchester United shirt when he took part in the 2-0 win over Liverpool in October 2006.

From here onwards he was not necessarily quite the permanent fixture in the team that he'd once been, but despite what you might call his advancing years, 2006-07 was a great year for Scholes. He put on a particularly fine display against Blackburn Rovers. United were losing 1-0, but Scholes turned the game around almost single-handedly and scored the equaliser. It ended 4-1 to the Reds and they won the League again.

◀ Goalscorer Paul Scholes is congratulated by Teddy Sheringham and Andy Cole of Manchester United during the AXA FA Cup Final match against Newcastle United played at Wembley Stadium. The match finished in a 2-0 win for Manchester United, 22 May 1999

▲ Scholes nets for United against Sunderland

◄ Messi can only watch as Manchester United's Paul Scholes scores against Barcelona during their UEFA Champions League second leg, 29 April 2008 at Old Trafford

In October 2007, he damaged knee ligaments the night before a Champions League group match against Dynamo Kyiv and was out until the following January. However, in April 2008 he made his hundredth Champions League appearance, away at Barcelona in the semi-finals first leg. That ended 0-0, but in the second leg Scholes scored the goal that took United to the final. Unfortunately he picked up a booking and an injury in the final against Chelsea, so came off just before full-time with the scores at 1-1. He missed extra-time, but picked up a winner's medal after United won the penalty shootout.

In May 2011 Scholes announced that he would be retiring as a player and was made a coach at Manchester United, but while training with the reserves he realised he missed playing. So in January 2012 he went back and did one more season on the field. He retired once again in May 2013, with his final appearance being in a game against West Bromwich Albion in which he came on as a sub and received a yellow card. It was the 97th of his career and, given that he was certainly no stranger to disciplinary action, perhaps a characteristic note to end on.

Part of that incredibly talented Class of '92 generation, as a player Scholes was physically compact and emotionally very calm and collected. He instinctively read the game well, so his movement was always intelligent. Technically he was strong, his passing was accurate and he was particularly well known for his late, attacking runs and his link play. He also had an excellent long-range shot on him. In the first half of his career he tended to play in the centre, but as he got older he moved to a deeper role, although he was just as incisive there as he had been in the middle of the pitch.

In 718 appearances for United, he scored 155 goals and won 25 trophies, including 11 league titles and two Champions League titles, and that was alongside a successful international career in which he was capped 66 times.

In 2019 he was briefly manager of Oldham Athletic and in 2020 briefly interim manager of Salford City, the club in which he, along with former teammates David Beckham, Nicky Butt, Ryan Giggs, Gary Neville and Phil Neville, had invested.

MARCUS RASHFORD

SPEED, TECHNICAL ABILITY AND A CERTAIN CALMNESS

A product of the Manchester United youth system, Marcus Rashford's innate talent and potential to make it to the top were identified at a very young age. He is an incredible asset to United, but equally he is immensely proud to be playing for the club he has always supported.

◀ Marcus Rashford 2019-20 Premier League Panini Trading Card

▶ Marcus Rashford celebrates victory after the Premier League match between Manchester City and Manchester United at Etihad Stadium on 7 December 2019

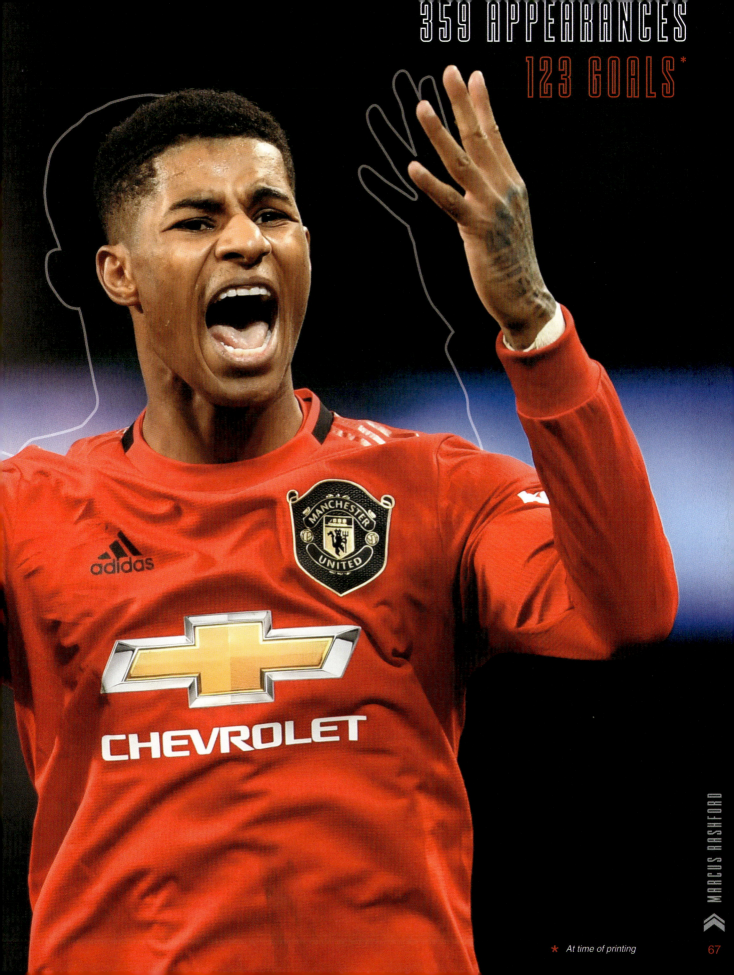

359 APPEARANCES
123 GOALS*

*At time of printing

MARCUS RASHFORD

▲ Marcus Rashford holds the trophy as the team pose for photos after The FA Community Shield match against Leicester at Wembley Stadium on 7 August 2016

Born in Manchester in 1997, Rashford's first team was Fletcher Moss Rangers. He was only five and played in goal, but even at that early age he stood out. He attracted interest from a number of clubs and trained with Manchester City for a week, before joining the Manchester United youth system at the age of seven — some of his family members were City supporters, but he has always been a United fan, so it wasn't surprising that he picked the Reds.

As a youngster he often missed training, because his mother, who was a single parent, and his older siblings were working and he couldn't get there. When staff at the club realised this, they arranged transport to the training ground for him. He showed such promise as a boy that he was fast-tracked and enrolled in the Schoolboy Scholars scheme at 11, a year early. The coaches also organised for him to improve his skills by playing cage football with players who were several years older than he was.

Rashford started attending first-team training when he was 16 and David Moyes was manager. He was then named as a sub for the first time in November 2014 when Louis van Gaal was in charge — Van Gaal had a strange superstition that all strikers should have a shirt number with a nine in it, so Rashford was allocated 39 — for a Premier League game against Watford. United won 2-1, but Rashford didn't come off the bench and he stayed there the following week, too, for a 1-1 draw against Leicester City.

Never mind, he was still very young, but he was

...THE YOUNGEST PLAYER EVER TO SCORE IN A MANCHESTER DERBY

gradually getting closer and closer to playing for the first team and finally made his team debut the following season, in February 2016. That was in a Europa League game against Danish side Midtjylland, which was also his European debut, and he made quite an impact by scoring twice in a 5-1 win.

In fact, he made a habit of scoring on debut, again getting two goals and an assist against Arsenal in his Premier League debut in the same month. He also scored in his League Cup and Champions League debuts, as well as in his first Manchester derby. Indeed, at the age of 18 years and 141 days he was actually the youngest player ever to score in a Manchester derby.

He was in the squad for the game against Midtjylland because United was in the midst of an injury crisis at the time, with 13 players unfit to play. That became 14 when Anthony Martial was injured during the warm-up, so Rashford was suddenly in the starting line-up. He impressed against Arsenal, with Van Gaal praising him extravagantly, but urging the media to give the young man the space to develop at his own pace. Then came that Manchester derby, when Rashford's goal was the only one in United's first away win over City for four years.

In that season's FA Cup, when, after a 1-1 draw, United had to replay their quarter-final game against West Ham, Rashford curled in a shot that helped his team win 2-1 and took them through to the semi-final against Everton, which United also won 2-1. Their opponents in the final were Crystal Palace and although he didn't get on the scoresheet, he played, United won 2-1 and he was presented with his first medal as a senior player. He finished the 2015-16 season having made 18 appearances and scored eight goals — not bad given his first game wasn't until February.

▶ Marcus Rashford celebrates scoring United's second goal during the Premier League match between Norwich City and Manchester United at Carrow Road, 27 October 2019

HE OFTEN SCORED AFTER COMING ON AS A SUB AND AT CRUCIAL MOMENTS

The new season brought two new faces to Old Trafford: manager José Mourinho, who assigned Rashford the number 19 shirt, signalling he had earned his place in the senior squad, and hugely experienced superstar striker Zlatan Ibrahimović, who often kept Rashford on the subs' bench or meant that Rashford was pushed out to the wing. In fact, Rashford scored his first goal of the season when he came on for Juan Mata against Hull City in late August. In September, he got one against Watford, one against Northampton Town in the League Cup and one against Leicester. However, that was followed by a dry period, but the drought ended in January when he got two in four minutes in an FA Cup game against Reading, which finished 4-0.

United met Southampton in the final of the League Cup in February and Rashford came on in the 77th minute. The Reds won 3-2. Having scored a key goal against Anderlecht in April, in the Europa League quarter-finals, in May he started in the final of the same competition against Ajax. Again, Manchester United won, this time 2-0. Rashford made 53 appearances over that 2016-17 season, more than any other United player, but scored a slightly disappointing 11 goals. Granted, he might have hoped for a higher tally, but it was still perfectly respectable given he rarely started games.

The Europa League trophy would prove to be the Reds' last for a while, but in terms of his own career the next couple of seasons were successful ones for Rashford. His number of appearances and goals remained broadly consistent, but he often scored quickly after coming on as a sub and often at crucial moments. For instance, in December 2017 he got the winner against CSKA Moscow and ensured that United qualified for the knockout phase of the Champions League, as well as being awarded man of the match.

The following December, now wearing the number 10 shirt, after Mourinho's departure and in Ole Gunnar Solskjær's first game as caretaker manager, he scored after just three minutes in a 5-1 trouncing of Cardiff City. In this period he also provided many crucial assists, and fellow players and pundits alike wondered at his composure and maturity, particularly as he was still very young. Indeed, in February 2019, at the age of 21 years and 95 days, he chalked up a hundred appearances for United (only Ryan Giggs has reached that milestone at a younger age) and celebrated by scoring the only goal of the game as the team beat Leicester City.

Rashford began 2019-20 emphatically by hitting two in a 4-0 win over Chelsea, but this was followed by a brief dip in form, before he hit the best goalscoring run of his career to date as he scored 16 in 20 games. Football was suspended for three months due to the Covid-19 pandemic, which more or less coincided with a long-term back injury for Rashford, so after 44 appearances his goal tally for the season was 22.

At the start of 2020-21 he continued to notch up goals, in October netting the winner away to PSG in the Champions League — it finished 2-1 — and then bagging his first hat-trick for United in a 5-0 win over RB Leipzig in the next game in the same competition. When playing Everton in November, though, he picked up a shoulder injury and the pain from that prompted an operation in April, which kept him out until October 2021. Inevitably he then seemed to struggle to find form, but he did come off the bench to score against Leicester and, as 2022 dawned, West Ham. Although not lacking in resilience, navigating that tricky spell was surely character-building and no doubt stiffened his resolve and will to win.

◀ Marcus Rashford scores his side's first goal during the Premier League match between Manchester United and Liverpool at Old Trafford on 20 October 2019

By the time the 2022-23 season began, United had a new manager, Erik ten Hag, the sixth Rashford had played under, and he began using Rashford as both a centre-forward and on the left wing. It was a good season for the team and they won their first silverware for several years when they lifted the League Cup. Rashford scored in every round of the competition with the exception of the semi-final second leg against Nottingham Forest at Old Trafford. He played in the final, too, in which they beat Newcastle United 2-0, and scored the second goal, although it was initially credited to Newcastle defender Sven Botman. Manchester United also met Manchester City in the 2023 FA Cup Final, but unfortunately lost 2-1 to City, with Rashford unable to make much impact on the game.

Rashford made his full England debut against Australia in May 2016 and, at 18, was the youngest Englishman to score on his international debut. He has over 50 caps and in 2021 became the seventh Manchester United player to captain England. He scored three goals in the 2022 World Cup, which matched Bobby Charlton's World Cup scoring record for a Manchester United player.

Athletic both running into space and on the ball, Marcus Rashford has speed, technical ability and a certain calmness, as well as an eye for the chance and superb finishing skills. He is also an excellent role model off the pitch as well as on it, and has been applauded for using his significant public profile as a footballer to campaign against racism, homelessness and, most prominently, child hunger. In 2020, he successfully lobbied the Government to extend its free school meals programme for children from low-income families to cover the summer holidays. To date, he has won the FA Cup, two League Cups and the Europa League with United, but he is still in his twenties and in the coming years there are surely many more trophies and titles in store for him and the club.

▼ Marcus Rashford 'takes a knee' in support of the No Room For Racism campaign ahead of the English Premier League football match between Manchester United and Manchester City at Old Trafford, 13 December 2020

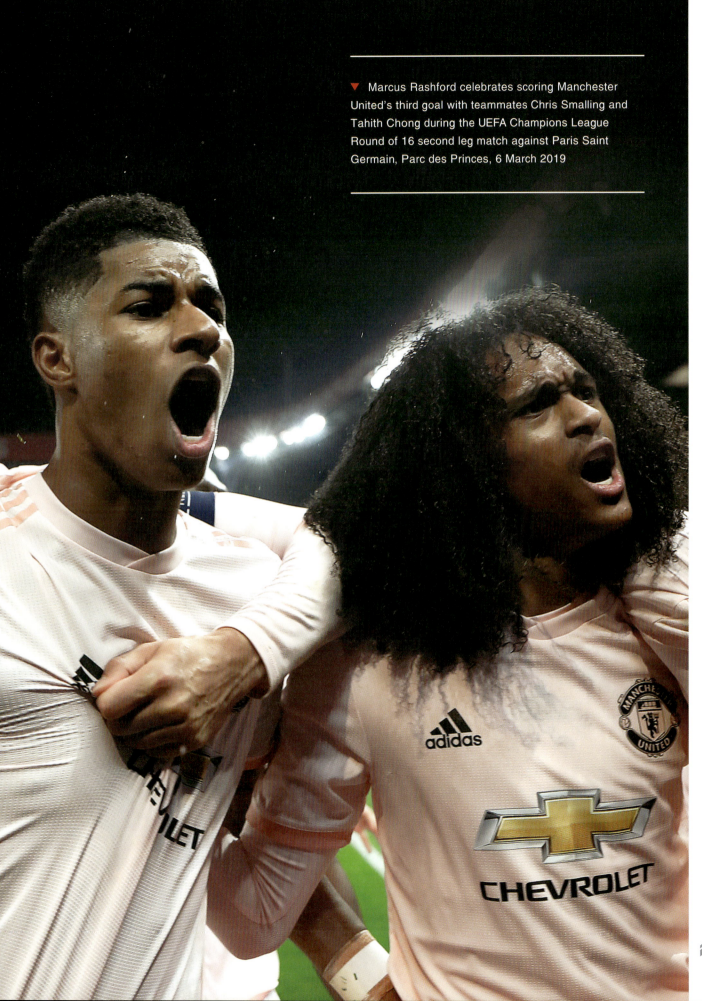

▼ Marcus Rashford celebrates scoring Manchester United's third goal with teammates Chris Smalling and Tahith Chong during the UEFA Champions League Round of 16 second leg match against Paris Saint Germain, Parc des Princes, 6 March 2019

WAYNE ROONEY

THE GOALS KEPT COMING AND THE RECORDS KEPT MOUNTING UP

Undoubtedly one of the best players of his or any generation, Wayne Rooney spent 13 incredibly successful years in a red shirt. Not only did he make 559 appearances for Manchester United, he is also the only player to have scored over 250 goals — 253 to be precise — for the club.

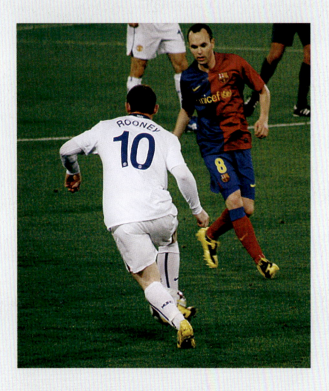

◀ Rooney takes on Andrés Iniesta of Barcelona during the 2009 UEFA Champions League Final

▶ Rooney and Ronaldo respond to Liverpool fans after Rooney scored during the Barclays Premiership match at Anfield, 15 January 2005

559 APPEARANCES
253 GOALS

WAYNE ROONEY

Born in Liverpool in 1985, Rooney joined Everton at the age of nine and made his professional debut for the club in 2002, when he was just 16. He spent two seasons playing for the club he had supported as a boy, before Alex Ferguson brought him to Manchester United in the summer of 2004 in a transfer deal worth £27 million. Rooney was still only 18 and it was the highest fee ever paid for a player under 20.

To say Rooney won everything is literally true, from the Premier League title, FA Cup and League Cup through to the Europa League and Champions League. With 53 goals in 120 international caps, he is England's second most-capped player and second top goalscorer. Although sometimes deployed as a creative midfielder, he spent much of his career as a centre-forward and, given he was such a prolific scorer, the story of his career with Manchester United can really be told through his goals.

He made his debut for the club in the number 8 shirt in late September 2004 in a Champions League 6-2 home win against Fenerbahçe, causing quite a stir by bagging himself a hat-trick. Although United failed

> **HIS CAREER WITH UNITED CAN REALLY BE TOLD THROUGH HIS GOALS**

◂ Wayne Rooney is congratulated after scoring against Everton during their Premiership match at Goodison Park, 28 April 2007

▸ Rooney during a Group D Champions League match against Sparta Prague in Prague, 19 October 2004

to win any honours in his first season at Old Trafford, Rooney did score 17 goals from 43 appearances in all competitions. His volley from the edge of the box against Middlesbrough in a January FA Cup game was chosen as BBC Goal of the Season and he was also made PFA Young Player of the Year.

The first trophy he won with United was the 2006 League Cup. The team's opponents in the final were Wigan Athletic and Rooney scored twice, as well as being named man of the match, in the Reds' 4-0 victory. Their Premier League title hopes were crushed, though, when they lost 3-0 away to eventual champions Chelsea. In the same game Rooney was tackled by Paulo Ferreira and sustained a broken metatarsal, but luckily he made a swift recovery and was back playing in six weeks.

However, at the start of the 2006-07 season he went ten games without a goal, before scoring a hat-trick away to Bolton Wanderers. Fast-forward to the end of that season and in April United were away at Everton, Rooney's former club. The home side were 2-0 up until the Red Devils fought back to level it and then Rooney got a third, kissing his shirt badge as he celebrated, igniting a long-running feud with Everton fans. He said he instantly regretted the action, but the Goodison Park crowd roundly booed him. It ended 4-2 to United, who went on to win the league title, with Rooney contributing 14 league goals.

He was now wearing the number 10 shirt, but fractured the metatarsal on his other foot on the opening day of the 2007-08 season. He was out for six weeks, came back, scored in early October against Roma in United's 1-0 Champions League group win, but damaged his ankle in training in early November and was out for another two weeks. Despite his absences, he chalked up 18 goals as United won not just the Premier League, but the Champions League too.

IT WAS AN OVERHEAD BICYCLE KICK THAT PROVED TO BE THE WINNER

Starting in 2005-06, the season after he arrived at Old Trafford, right up until 2012-13, Manchester United came either first or second in the Premier League and, despite suffering his fair share of injuries, Rooney was at the heart of all those campaigns.

On 4 October 2008, in an away win over Blackburn Rovers, he became the youngest player to make 200 Premier League appearances. On 14 January 2009 he scored against Wigan Athletic after 54 seconds, but had to go off seven minutes later with a pulled hamstring. Then in the May he played in the Champions League Final against Barcelona in Rome, although United lost 2-0.

In the first league game of the 2009-10 season, which was against Birmingham City, he scored the only goal, taking his United total to 99, and then less than a week later, against Wigan, he got two, making him the 20th Manchester United player to score a hundred goals.

In November, he got his first hat-trick for three years in a 4-1 away win against Portsmouth and in January 2010, when United met Hull City, he got all four of the goals in a 4-0 victory. He ended the season with 34 goals from 44 appearances, and also won the Professional Footballers' Association Players' Player of the Year and the Football Writers' Association Footballer of the Year.

At the start of the 2010-11 season, Alex Ferguson made it known that Rooney wanted to leave United.

◀ Wayne Rooney scores what he deemed his greatest goal – an overhead kick in the Premier League match against Manchester City at Old Trafford, 12 February 2011

Rooney had recently been dropped from the side. Ferguson insisted this was due to an ankle injury, but Rooney disputed that. However, the argument was suddenly sorted out and Rooney signed a new five-year contract, taking him through to June 2015.

Once he was playing again he continued to score and to contribute lots of valuable assists, but in February 2011 he hit a goal that won the Premier League 20 Seasons Awards Best Goal. In the Manchester derby, it was an overhead bicycle kick that proved to be the winner in a 2-1 victory. Afterwards, Rooney described it as the best of his career. In May that year, in the season's penultimate game, he converted a penalty to equalise for United against Blackburn Rovers. The game ended in a 1-1 draw, but the point secured another league title — a record 19th for the club.

The goals kept coming and the records kept mounting up for Rooney in 2011-12. In late August, he scored his 150th goal for United, number one of three in a game in which they beat Arsenal 8-2. He then got another hat-trick in early September against Bolton Wanderers, making him only the fourth player in Premier League history to score a hat-trick in consecutive games. In October, he netted twice in a Champions League fixture against Otelul Galati, taking the record for the highest-scoring Englishman in Champions League history from former United player Paul Scholes.

On the last day of the season, United were playing Sunderland and Rooney put the Red Devils ahead. Also in the running for the Premier League title were Manchester City, who were losing 2-1 to Queens Park Rangers, so Rooney's winner looked like it would be decisive. However, Manchester City scored twice in injury time to make it 3-2 and take the title. United's season ended trophyless.

STOCKHOLM FINAL 2017

That was rectified the following season, though. City were the chief rivals once again, but by the time the final whistle of the final game blew, United were 11 points clear. It was Alex Ferguson's last season in charge and he went out with a bang, although before he did he announced that Rooney had put in a transfer request.

Once Ferguson had retired, several other clubs, including PSG and Real Madrid, registered their interest in buying Rooney, but new manager David Moyes told them he was not for sale. In February 2014 he signed a contract extension that would keep him at Old Trafford until 2019 and, despite the fact that the next couple of seasons weren't United's most successful, he went on scoring, finishing 2013-14 as top scorer with 19 goals in all competitions and 2014-15 as top scorer again, this time with 14 goals.

Ahead of the 2014-15 season, and after the departure of Vidić, another new manager, Louis van Gaal, had made Rooney club captain, although he tended to use Rooney as more of a midfielder, which may have resulted in a slightly lower goal haul. In 2015-16 his total was 15, but Anthony Martial bested him with 18. However, 2016 was an FA Cup-winning year and, although Rooney didn't score in the final against Crystal Palace — United won 2-1 after extra-time — he was

◀ Wayne Rooney lifts the trophy, following the UEFA Europa League Final match against Ajax at Friends Arena, 24 May 2017

▼ Rooney receiving an award for becoming Manchester United's record goalscorer from previous record holder Sir Bobby Charlton in January 2017

named man of the match and had been crucial to the team's progress along the road to Wembley.

After 13 years at Old Trafford, the 2016-17 season was to be Rooney's last, but that didn't stop him achieving a significant milestone. On 7 January he scored against Reading in the FA Cup to equal Bobby Charlton's record of 249 goals for the club, although Rooney reached that number 215 matches and four seasons faster than Charlton. Then on 21 January Rooney took a free kick to score an equaliser away to Stoke City and passed Charlton's total. Fittingly, it was Charlton who presented Rooney with a Golden Boot to mark his achievement before a 29 January game against Wigan Athletic.

In February, when United beat Southampton 3-2 to win another League Cup, Rooney was a sub, but didn't come off the bench. In May, though, in his final game for the Red Devils, he did come on as United won the Europa League by beating Ajax 2-0. It was quite a highpoint to end on. After leaving Old Trafford, Rooney returned to former club Everton for a season, before moving to DC United, the Washington DC-based Major League Soccer (MLS) team, for a year. He then went to Derby County as player-manager and then manager, subsequently moving back to DC United as manager.

CRISTIANO RONALDO

OTHER CLUBS WERE CIRCLING, SO UNITED ACTED SWIFTLY

Naturally right-footed, yet able to play on either wing or as a striker, Cristiano Ronaldo is famous for his flicks and tricks — and maybe his showboating too. A supreme stylist, elegant but with a powerful shot on him, he loved playing for Manchester United so much he came back.

▼ Cristiano Ronaldo receives his Player of the Month award alongside Alex Ferguson who picked up the Manager of the Month, April 2008

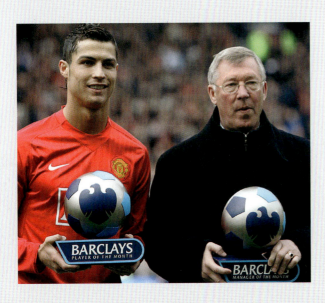

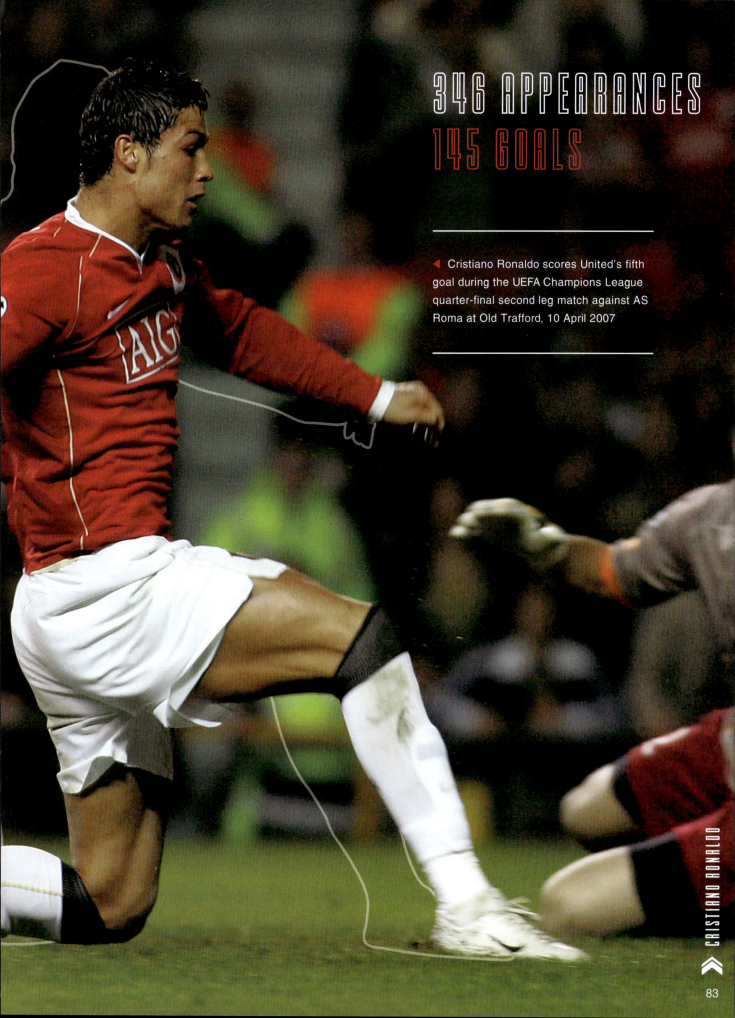

346 APPEARANCES
145 GOALS

◀ Cristiano Ronaldo scores United's fifth goal during the UEFA Champions League quarter-final second leg match against AS Roma at Old Trafford, 10 April 2007

HE WAS THE MOST EXPENSIVE TEENAGER IN ENGLISH FOOTBALLING HISTORY

Cristiano Ronaldo, born in 1985 on the Portuguese island of Madeira, arrived in Manchester in August 2003. He was 18 and had been playing for Sporting CP in Portugal, having joined its youth academy at age 12. Legend has it that on the plane back from a pre-season friendly with Sporting, the players, impressed with his raw talent, convinced Alex Ferguson he should buy Ronaldo. The truth is the youngster had been on the manager's radar for a while. However, other clubs were circling, so United acted swiftly and for a fee of £12.24 million Ronaldo came to Old Trafford. At the time, he was the most expensive teenager in English footballing history.

Although he had asked for number 28, the same number he'd had at Sporting, instead he was given 7 – as worn by Best, Cantona and Beckham. Presumably Ferguson calculated that the fact that those great names had previously worn the shirt would motivate Ronaldo further. Ronaldo undoubtedly had talent, but it was fairly raw, and Ferguson was crucial to his development, understanding exactly how to get the best out of him. His initials combined with his shirt number also led to his nickname, and indeed global brand, CR7.

Ronaldo made his debut as a sub, coming on for Nicky Butt in a 4-0 home win over Bolton Wanderers in the league on 16 August. He scored his first goal for the club from a free kick in a 3-0 win over Portsmouth on 1 November. He followed that up with three more league goals, including one against Aston Villa on the last day of the season, a game in which he also sent off for the first time in his career. His goal tally for his initial season with Manchester United was six and perhaps that was slightly disappointing, but it did include the opener in the FA Cup Final. United faced Millwall and won 3-0. Ronaldo had his first winners' medal and it wouldn't be his last.

United's thousandth goal in the Premier League was scored by Ronaldo at the end of October 2004, in a game they lost 4-1 to Middlesbrough, and he had clearly proved his value as shortly afterwards his contract was extended by two years, through to 2010. The team reached the 2005 FA Cup Final, where they faced Arsenal, but it was goalless after extra-time. Ronaldo converted his penalty, but United ultimately lost 4-5, and he ended the season having made 50 appearances and scored nine goals.

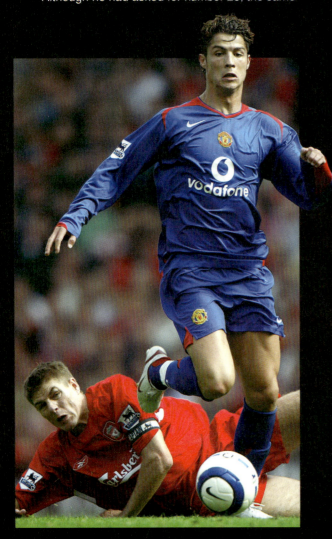

◀ Cristiano Ronaldo races away after evading the challenge of Steven Gerrard

◀ Cristiano Ronaldo of Manchester United during the FA Barclaycard Premiership match between Chelsea and Manchester United at Stamford Bridge, 30 November 2003

▲ Nani and Cristiano Ronaldo with the Champions League trophy at Luzhniki Stadium in Moscow, 21 May 2008

However, he didn't have to wait too long for another trophy, because in February 2006, United won the League Cup, beating Wigan Athletic 4-0. Ronaldo got the third goal, just before the hour was up — Wigan lost the ball in midfield to Louis Saha, who passed to an unmarked Ronaldo, who slotted it away elegantly.

There were also some controversial episodes during that season as UEFA gave him a one-match ban for making a rude gesture to Benfica fans and he was sent off in a Manchester derby for kicking former United player Andrew Cole. It was a World Cup year, 2006, and he was also involved in an unfortunate altercation with club teammate Wayne Rooney, which led to Rooney being sent off. Ronaldo complained about United's lack of support over the incident and made a public transfer request, but the club refused to consider it.

Consequently, Ronaldo was consistently booed by fans all the next season, but arguably that only motivated him more as it turned out to be his breakout year. At this time he was doing a lot of work on a one-to-one basis with Dutch first-team coach René Meulensteen, who helped him become more of a team player.

He also encouraged him to be less predictable on the field, calling for the ball and making chances, rather than hanging around waiting for the perfect opportunity to score the perfect goal. Meulensteen certainly deserves some of the credit for improvements in Ronaldo's game and by the end of 2006-07 not only had he scored 23 in 53 appearances, but United had won the league title.

AS 2008 ENDED HE WON THE FIRST OF HIS FIVE BALLON D'OR AWARDS

The 2007-08 season proved to be a massive one for both United and Ronaldo. He made 49 appearances and scored an incredible 42 goals in all competitions. By mid-September United were top of the league and they stayed in first or second position right through until May. At the end of September Ronaldo got a goal away at Birmingham and from that point onwards he scored consistently in almost every league match, again, right through until May. One of the highpoints was a hat-trick, his first for United, in a 6-0 trouncing of Newcastle United in January, and in March he captained the Red Devils for the first time and scored both goals in a 2-0 win over Bolton Wanderers.

Manchester United won the league title for the second time in a row. They also won the Champions League. Ronaldo was instrumental in their journey to the final — he was the Champions League top scorer — and he netted United's normal-time goal when they met Chelsea in Moscow. However, at 1-1 it went to extra-time and then penalties. Unaccountably, Ronaldo, usually so confident, had his shot saved by Chelsea keeper Petr Čech. It looked like all was lost, but fortunately John Terry hit the post. In the event, it went to sudden-death penalties, Nicolas Anelka missed and Chelsea lost.

Before the start of the 2008-09 season, Ronald had surgery on his ankle and was out for ten weeks, but on his return he scored his hundredth goal for the Red Devils in a 5-0 victory over Stoke City. As 2008 ended he won the first of his five Ballon d'Or awards, as chosen by international sports journalists, and as 2009 dawned he was made FIFA World Player of the Year as well. United won the league cup and a third consecutive league title, and Ronaldo made 53 appearances and chalked up 26 goals. His last was from a free kick at home to City in the Manchester derby.

▶ Cristiano Ronaldo congratulates Wayne Rooney during the FIFA Club World Cup Japan 2008 Final match against Liga De Quito at the International Stadium Yokohama, Kanagawa, 21 December 2008

◀ Cristiano Ronaldo in a Premier League match against Newcastle in September 2021, his first game back at Manchester United

▶ CR7 certainly did the famous number 7 shirt proud following the likes of Beckham, Cantona and Best

Cristiano Ronaldo subsequently spent nine seasons at Real Madrid and three at Juventus until, in August 2021, he re-signed for Manchester United on a two-year contract worth £12.85. Edinson Cavani, who at the time was wearing 7, was persuaded to switch to 21, so Ronaldo could pull on his old shirt number. In the first 24 hours after Ronaldo's return was announced, sales of replica shirts went through the roof.

On his second Old Trafford debut, on 11 September 2021, he scored the first two goals in a 4-1 league victory over Newcastle, which was a pretty emphatic way to say he was back. On 29 September and 20 October he got last-minute winners in the Champions League against, respectively, Villarreal and Atalanta, and then scored a last-minute equaliser in the Atalanta return fixture on 2 November. Another goal in the other Villareal leg meant he was the first English club player to net in five consecutive Champions League matches.

On 2 December, Ronaldo came away from a 3-2 league win against Arsenal with two goals and at the same time he passed the 800 career goals mark, but after that his performances, and the team's, steadily deteriorated. He went two months without scoring, next hitting the back of the net in mid-February in a game against Brighton and Hove Albion, which United won 2-0, but was then out for a month with a hamstring injury. The records kept coming, though, and in April he achieved his fiftieth club hat-trick in a 3-2 victory over Norwich City and his hundredth Premier League goal in a 3-1 loss to Arsenal.

He ended the season on 24 goals in total, but his relationship with interim manager Ralf Rangnick had become increasingly strained, and he was more and more unhappy about what he perceived as the club's direction on and off the pitch. He missed the pre-season tour of Thailand and Australia due to a family matter, but incoming manager Erik ten Hag insisted that he was very much part of the club's future plans. Meanwhile, Ronaldo's agent began to seek a transfer deal, but although he played in Europa League games, in the league he was being used as a substitute, which made Ronaldo even more disgruntled.

This culminated in October, when Ronaldo refused to go on as a sub against Tottenham Hotspur and left Old Trafford before the full-time whistle had gone. It was clear that Ronaldo was at breaking point and in November gave an interview to journalist Piers Morgan in which he was highly critical of the club and Ten Hag. It therefore came as no surprise to fans when, on 22 November, his contract was terminated by mutual agreement, effective immediately. It was a somewhat disappointing end to a glorious relationship with the Red Devils, perhaps proving that you should never go back. In January 2023, a few weeks shy of his 38th birthday, he joined Saudi Arabian club Al-Nassr on a two-year contract.

TOP 50 GREATEST PLAYERS OF ALL TIME

The players featured over the coming pages were all — and in some cases still are — exceptional footballers and all have played a crucial role in Manchester United's incredible success on the pitch, whether that's helping the club win domestic honours or being part of sides that have won international trophies. Some are household names, others are less well known, but they all showed an unfaltering commitment to the club and proudly pulled on the famous red shirt.

▶ Manchester United: a club full of legends

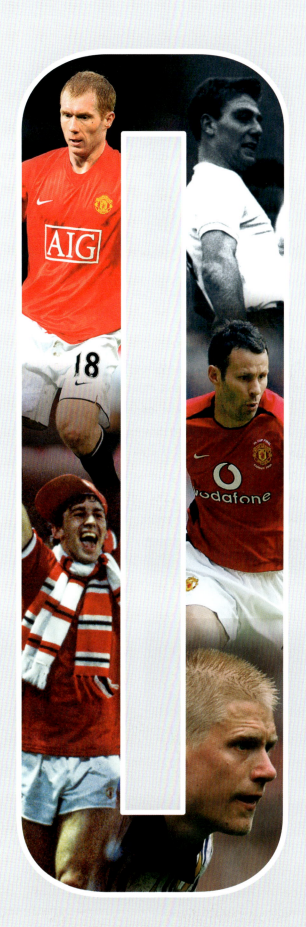

TOP 50 GREATEST PLAYERS OF ALL TIME

50 > BRIAN KIDD

A Mancunian by birth, striker Brian Kidd joined the Manchester United academy in 1964, aged 15, turning professional three years later. He always had a good eye for goal and on his 19th birthday memorably scored a header during extra time in the 1968 European Cup Final, in which United beat Benfica 4-1. In 203 league appearances for United he scored 52 times, but in 1974 he left to go to Arsenal, later playing for several other clubs, including Manchester City. In the 90s, though, he returned to United as an assistant to manager Alex Ferguson and was instrumental in the development of the young Double-winning side.

48 > TEDDY SHERINGHAM

Striker Teddy Sheringham was signed from Spurs as a 1997 replacement for Eric Cantona and, despite his relative maturity (he was 31) was an integral part of the Treble-winning team of 1998-99. That season he helped United win the league, lift the FA Cup after scoring in the 2-0 victory over Newcastle United, and repeated that feat in the 2-1 win over Bayern Munich in the Champions League Final. The following year he won a second Premiership title with United and the year after that a third, playing some of the best football of his career. In all, he made 104 appearances for the club and scored 31 goals, returning to Glenn Hoddle's Tottenham on a free transfer in 2001.

49 > STAN PEARSON

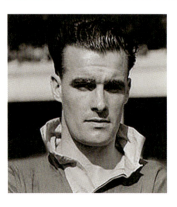

Inside-forward Stan Pearson was a key member of Matt Busby's first great team; the team that won the 1948 FA Cup — Pearson scored when they beat Blackpool 4-2 in the final — and won the league in 1952. Born in Salford, he was scouted while playing for Adelphi Lads' Club and signed as an amateur in 1935, becoming a professional two years later. Unfortunately, his career was interrupted by the Second World War, but he picked it up again when matches resumed in 1946 and was a first-team regular for the Red Devils until 1953. He had a powerful shot, was very reliable, and partnered well with Jack Rowley.

47 > JOHNNY CAREY

Irishman John Carey played for Manchester United both before and after the Second World War, making 304 appearances and scoring 17 goals between 1936 and 1953. However, he also played 112 games and scored 47 times for the club, and made a handful of guest spots for other clubs too, during the war itself, in the regional wartime leagues. A versatile defensive midfielder, after the war, under Matt Busby's management, he captained the team to their 4-2 victory over Blackpool in the 1948 Cup Final as well as their 1952 First Division title.

46 GARY PALLISTER

Gary Pallister and fellow centre-back Steve Bruce formed what was probably United's greatest-ever defensive partnership. Fast, skilful on the ball and good in the air, Pallister was with the club almost a decade, from 1989 to 1998, and in that time he made 317 league appearances and won four Premiership titles, three FA Cups, one League Cup, one European Cup-Winners' Cup and a European Super Cup. He didn't score many goals — 12 in his career with the team — but those he did were often crucial, like the two he got against Liverpool at Anfield which settled the 1996-97 title race in United's favour.

44 BRUNO FERNANDES

The club reportedly paid £67.7 million for Portuguese player Bruno Fernandes when he was signed from Sporting Lisbon in 2020, but the attacking midfielder has undoubtedly proved his worth. A great playmaker capable of piercing passes and a clinical penalty-taker, he's demonstrated his versatility by playing on both the right and centrally. A commanding captain, he can also take up a deeper position when asked to by his manager and no one could fault his work rate. To date, he has scored over 100 goals in more than a 150 appearances for the Red Devils in all competitions.

45 HARRY GREGG

A United player from 1957 until 1966, goalkeeper Harry Gregg made 247 appearances and kept a clean sheet in 48 of them. Originally from Northern Ireland, he was at Doncaster Rovers for five years before Matt Busby bought him for £23,000 — at the time a world record transfer fee for a keeper. However, beyond his prowess on the field, Gregg is remembered because in 1958 he was involved in the Munich air disaster and pulled several teammates, including Bobby Charlton, the seriously injured Busby and other passengers from the burning wreckage. After a stellar career at United, he eventually retired due to a long-standing shoulder injury and went into management.

43 JACK ROWLEY

Jack Rowley arrived at Old Trafford in 1937, aged 17, and scored 18 goals in his first season, helping United return to Division One, before the Second World War intervened. Although bought as an outside-left, after the war, under Matt Busby's direction, he became a very effective centre-forward, forming strong partnerships with Stan Pearson and Scotsman Jimmy Delaney. He had a legendary left foot and was nicknamed the Gunner for his sharp shooting, scoring twice in the 1948 FA Cup Final 4-2 victory over Blackpool. When he eventually left the club in 1954, he had made an astounding 503 appearances and hit 312 goals.

42 ANDREW COLE

It was quite a shock when Kevin Keegan's Newcastle suddenly sold Andrew Cole to United for a record £6.25 million, but despite arriving in January 1995, he still got 12 goals in 18 games. However, his first two full seasons did not go smoothly and it wasn't until 1997-98, when Cantona had retired, that Cole became first-choice striker and found his best form, and when Dwight Yorke arrived from Villa in 1998 he and Cole formed a legendary strike partnership. A strong all-founder renowned for his finishing, Cole won eight trophies in six years at United, scoring consistently season after season until he left for Blackburn Rovers in January 2001.

40 LUKE SHAW

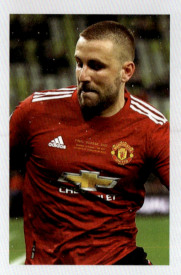

In 2014, when Luke Shaw signed for United from Southampton for £30 million, he was 19 and said to be the most expensive teenager in the world, but Luke Shaw has proved to be a first-team regular and true asset to the club. He's a left-back, but an attacking left-back who can also play centre-half. He's fast and thinks on his feet, and to date he's won the 2016 Community Shield, the 2017 Europa League and the 2023 League Cup with United. That initial contract has been renewed twice and Shaw should remain a United player until at least 2027.

41 JAAP STAM

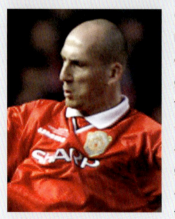

Generally held to be one of the best defenders of his generation, if not all time, Dutchman Jaap Stam was strong, fast, and a centre-back with great positional sense and a real ability to play the ball. Previously at PSV Eindhoven, he was bought for £10.5 million and spent three seasons at United, from 1998 to 2001. In that time he scored a single goal, but won three league titles, the FA Cup and the Champions League, plus the Intercontinental Cup. Ferguson later admitted that selling him to Lazio, albeit for a fee in excess of £15 million, was a mistake.

39 PAUL INCE

Central midfielder Paul Ince arrived at Old Trafford from Upton Park in 1989 amid some controversy — he was photographed in a United shirt well before the transfer deal was actually signed and West Ham fans didn't like it. However, he quickly settled down and became a stalwart of Alex Ferguson's first great side. On the field "the Guv'nor" was focused, aggressive even, and able to switch effortlessly from defence to attack. He won two Premier League titles, two FA Cups, a League Cup and a European Cup-Winners' Cup with United, making 281 appearances and bagging 28 goals in all competitions, before he was sold to Inter Milan for £7.5 million in 1995.

38 — MICHAEL CARRICK

Michael Carrick was bought from Tottenham in 2006 to fill the boots of Roy Keane. No pressure, then, but he quickly became a commanding presence in midfield. A stylish passer of the ball, he was always versatile, but particularly comfortable playing deep. He had several periods of injury, but United won five league championships, one FA Cup and the Champions League in his time. In all he made 464 appearances and scored 24 goals. His playing career ended in 2017-18, but he stayed at United and had a brief but successful stint as caretaker manager after Solskjær's departure, before finally leaving the club in late 2021.

37 — TONY DUNNE

The Irish left-back Tony Dunne arrived at Manchester United in 1960 and was part of the side Matt Busby built after the Munich air disaster, helping the team win the FA Cup in 1963, league titles in 1965 and 1967, and the European Cup in 1968. As a defender he was pacey and courageous, and he made 535 appearances for the club over a period of 13 years. In July 1973 he left the Red Devils on a free transfer and went to Bolton Wanderers, where he played 170 games. He died in 2020, aged 78.

36 — STEVE COPPELL

Steve Coppell was playing part-time for Tranmere Rovers and studying for a degree in economic history at Liverpool University when Tommy Docherty invited him to move to Manchester United. He accepted — as long as he could finish his degree — and made his debut in March 1975. Fast, direct and with excellent ball control, after that he was pretty much ever-present in the United side. It was not an era laden with honours for United, but he was a 1977 FA Cup winner. He had to miss the 1983 Cup Final due to injury and retired that year, at only 28, but went on to have a long managerial career.

35 ▸ PAUL MCGRATH

Irishman Paul McGrath was usually a centre-back, but could also play as a defensive midfielder. He came to United in 1982 and during Ron Atkinson's time in charge he was a first-team regular, usually partnered with Kevin Moran in the centre of defence. However, when Atkinson was replaced by Alex Ferguson in 1986 he started to fall out of favour, partly due to competition from new signings such as Mal Donaghy and Steve Bruce, and partly due problems with his knees. He left for Aston Villa in 1989, but is remembered at United for his pace, power and cool head.

34 ▸ BRIAN MCCLAIR

Scottish striker Brian McClair spent 11 seasons at Manchester United. In 1987-88, his debut season, he bagged 24 goals and went on to score 127 in a total of 471 appearances. He had a highly productive partnership with Mark Hughes, and won 14 titles and trophies with the club. In 1994 he was part of the club's first Double-winning team and as substitute scored the final goal in the FA Cup Final 4-0 defeat of Chelsea. After he retired as a player, McClair worked as a coach at Blackburn Rovers before returning to Manchester United, where he was director of the youth academy for several years.

33 ▸ OLE GUNNAR SOLSKJÆR

In 1996, when Ferguson signed Norwegian striker Ole Gunnar Solskjær, he was unknown, but after 11 years, 366 appearances and 126 goals everyone knew him. United enjoyed massive success during his era and he was at the heart of that success. "The Baby-faced Assassin" had many career highlights and was notable for never giving up, often scoring late in games when it really mattered. In the 1999 Champions League final against Bayern Munich he was a substitute and flicked the ball into the top of the net in stoppage time to clinch the Treble. He also made a significant contribution to the club as caretaker and then permanent manager from 2018 to 2021.

32 ▸ EDWIN VAN DER SAR

Goalkeepers don't get many assists, but in the first minute of a 2011 league game against Aston Villa, an astute Edwin van der Sar targeted Wayne Rooney with a long pass. Rooney picked the ball up and shot straight past Brad Friedel in the Villa goal to score. That level of awareness made the Dutchman one of the greatest keepers of all time. A vital component of Ferguson's successful side of the late 2000s, Van der Sar was with United for six years, from 2005 to 2011, retiring, age 40, after 266 appearances and ten trophies.

31 PATRICE EVRA

Lauded as one of the best full-backs of his generation, Frenchman Patrice Evra arrived from Monaco in 2006 and left for Juventus in 2014. Although it took him a couple of seasons to become a first-team regular, he played 379 games for the club in all competitions and won 15 trophies. Known as a character both in the dressing room and on the field, not only was he strong, fast and technically gifted, he was clearly passionate about being a United player. He is also remembered for a 2012 incident in which he was racially abused by Liverpool's Luis Suárez, who was subsequently banned for eight matches.

30 MARTIN BUCHAN

At the heart of Manchester United's team in the 1970s was Scottish centre-half Martin Buchan. He spent 11 years at the club, from 1972 to 1983, and was captain for six of them. After the shock relegation to Division Two in 1973-74, in 1974-75 Buchan led the side to the Second Division title and straight back to the First Division. He also captained them to the 2-1 victory against Liverpool in the 1977 FA Cup Final. In his 456 appearances for the Red Devils, he was always composed with strong positional awareness, but he was also capable of bursts of pace and even scored four goals.

29 STEVE BRUCE

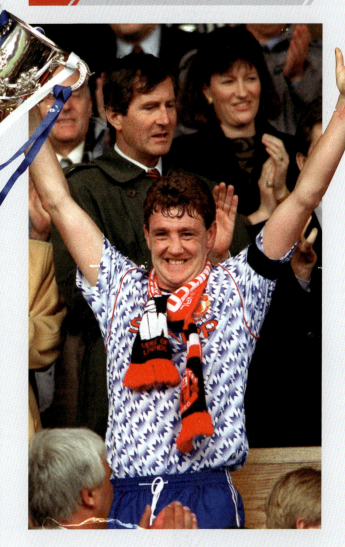

The adjective "uncompromising" is often used about centre-half Steve Bruce and he certainly made an impact when he arrived in Manchester in 1987. Indeed, the sides that won the 1992-93, 1993-94 and 1995-96 League titles, the 1994 and 1996 FA Cups, the 1992 League Cup and the 1991 European Cup-Winners' Cup were founded on his central defensive partnership with Gary Pallister and his leadership. In 414 appearances for United he scored an impressive 51 goals, including several penalties and two late headers against Sheffield Wednesday in a game that effectively gave the Red Devils the 1992-93 Premiership title. When he left United in 1996 he played for a number of other clubs before embarking on a managerial career.

28 RUUD VAN NISTELROOY

Ruud van Nistelrooy was a goal machine for Manchester United. At the end of his five years at Old Trafford he had made 219 appearances and scored 150 goals. The Dutchman arrived in 2001 and his first three seasons in Manchester were his best – he netted 36, 44 and 30 times respectively. Injury dogged his fourth season, although he still scored 16 and was Champions League top scorer with eight, and in his fifth he got on the scoresheet 24 times. By then, however, he was falling out of favour, with Louis Saha taking his place in the team. He left in 2006, bound for Real Madrid.

27 PADDY CRERAND

Definitely up there with the greatest midfielders ever to wear the red shirt, Scotsman Pat Crerand came to United from Celtic and his time in Manchester – he made 401 appearances between 1963 and 1971 – coincided with an incredibly exciting era. He was part of the teams that won the league title twice, the FA Cup and the European Cup. You couldn't exactly call him fast, but he was known for his tenacity and his hard tackles. He was also able to pass the ball forward accurately, creating chances for the likes of Best and Charlton to latch on to.

26 MARK HUGHES

Mark Hughes had two glorious spells at United. After joining the club in 1980, he made his first-team debut in 1983. He then partnered Frank Stapleton upfront and in 1984-85 was part of the FA Cup-winning side, but a contract issue saw him depart to Barcelona, at that time managed by Terry Venables, in 1986. He returned to Manchester, via Bayern Munich, in 1988, and this time stayed until 1995. Hughes and the Frenchman Eric Cantona were a truly explosive partnership and in that period he won numerous honours, including the Double in 1993-94. Always a player who knew his own mind, Hughes was a brilliant striker who unfailingly rose to the occasion.

25 NORMAN WHITESIDE

Born and raised in Belfast, Norman Whiteside had extraordinary natural talent and signed professional papers with United in 1982, when he was 17. In the next seven years he made 274 appearances for the club, scoring 74 goals and picking up FA Cup-winners medals in 1983 and 1985. He played as a forward and, when Frank Stapleton and Mark Hughes formed an effective striking partnership, a midfielder. Whiteside wasn't necessarily speedy, but he was certainly quick-witted and had a good shot on him. In 1989 he moved to Everton, but a knee injury forced him to retire a couple of years later at the age of just 26.

24 DENNIS VIOLLET

A local lad, from the Fallowfield area of Manchester, Dennis Viollet joined the club as an amateur, turning professional in 1953 at the age of 17. He forged a powerful partnership with Tommy Taylor — Viollet brought finesse, Taylor provided the muscle — and the Busby Babes won consecutive league championships in 1956 and 1957. The following season Viollet scored in the European Cup quarter-final against Red Star Belgrade and was on the plane home with the rest of the team, but sustained only minor head injuries in the crash. He was a great striker and his 293 appearances for United resulted in 179 goals. He left for Stoke City in 1962 and died in 1999.

23 DAVID DE GEA

The Spaniard has made over 500 appearances for the Red Devils since arriving from Atlético Madrid in summer 2011 for a transfer fee of £18.9 million (at the time a British record for a goalkeeper) and he has won a host of honours with the club, including a Premier League title, FA Cup and the UEFA Europa League. David de Gea has all the attributes needed by a keeper: he is tall but agile, uses his feet just as effectively as his hands and is a commanding presence on the pitch. In fact, he is generally considered to be one of the best keepers in the business and for United he has certainly proved that time and time again.

22 NOBBY STILES

Norbert — Nobby — Stiles had a reputation as a hardman, but as a defensive midfielder he was unrivalled. He also had an incredibly quick footballing mind and could time a pass from the back perfectly. Small, nippy and with a distinctive toothless smile when he took his dentures out to play, the European Cup final against Benfica in 1968 was probably his finest hour, but in the 11 years he spent at United, from 1960 to 1971, he also won league titles in 1965 and 1967. He scored 19 goals for the club in 395 appearances, went on to play for Middlesbrough and Preston North End, and had a career as a manager as well. He died in 2020.

21　RIO FERDINAND

For 12 seasons, centre-back Rio Ferdinand was pretty much ever-present in Manchester United's back line, forming a defensive partnership with Nemanja Vidić that opposition players found hard to beat. In fact, between 2002 and 2014 he picked up six league titles, two League Cups and a European Cup with the club, although he missed the 2004 FA Cup victory due to an eight-month ban for failing to stay for a drugs test. Poised and with a sharp turn of speed, in 455 appearances for United he only scored eight goals, but got a notable late winner in Alex Ferguson's final game at Old Trafford before retirement. When Ferdinand left football, he became a TV pundit.

19　NEMANJA VIDIĆ

Alex Ferguson reportedly pursued Serbian centre-back Nemanja Vidić for more than two years before, in January 2006, he finally brought him to Old Trafford from Spartak Moscow for a transfer fee of £7 million. However, it was worth the wait, because once installed in Manchester Vidić formed a legendary and highly effective defensive partnership with Rio Ferdinand. He won various honours with the team and some would argue he was the best defender to ever play for the club — he was certainly focused and extremely dependable. At the end of the 2013-14 season he moved to Inter Milan on a free transfer, but retired a couple of years later.

20　BILL FOULKES

Bill Foulkes was a great defender and a great servant of Manchester United. He played for the club for 18 years, making his first-team debut in 1952. He was lucky enough to avoid serious injury in the 1958 Munich air disaster and captained the team in its immediate aftermath. When the Red Devils finally won the European Cup in 1968, he and Bobby Charlton were the only crash survivors left at the club. Foulkes started out as a right-back, before moving to centre-half, but was never a big scorer, averaging one goal every two seasons, but made a staggering total of 688 appearances.

18　DENIS IRWIN

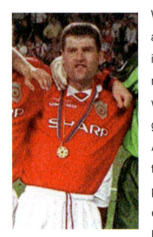

With 529 appearances and, for a full-back, an impressive 33 goals to his name, Irishman Denis Irwin was another contender for greatest ever defender and Alex Ferguson is alleged to have described him as, pound for pound, his greatest ever signing — he was bought from Oldham Athletic in 1990 for just £625,000. Irwin spent 12 years at Old Trafford, winning seven league titles, two FA Cups, the League Cup, the Champions League and the European Cup-Winners' Cup. He was comfortable playing on either the left or the right, and was something of a free kick and penalty specialist. He left the club in 2002 and post-retirement he has worked in the media.

17 TOMMY TAYLOR

When Matt Busby signed Tommy Taylor it was for a transfer fee of £29,999 — Busby knocked £1 off the deal, because he thought being a £30,000 player would be a burden. This was in 1953 and although Taylor wasn't technically a Busby Babe, having first played for his hometown team, Barnsley, he was nonetheless part of that generation and, tragically, was one of the eight players who died in the Munich air disaster. He was only 26, but had indisputably made his mark as a great centre-forward who had excellent control, could pass the ball with pinpoint accuracy and headed the ball beautifully, scoring 131 goals in 191 appearances.

16 ROGER BYRNE

A Manchester native, Busby Babe Roger Byrne made his first-team debut for the Red Devils in 1951, quickly becoming a regular and then, in the mid-1950s, captain. He was a full-back, although Matt Busby tried to play him as an outside-left, but he was uncomfortable there and engineered a return to his preferred position. Athletic and agile, charismatic and calm, he made 245 appearances for United and won three league titles, in 1952, 1956 and 1957, leading the team to the two latter successes. However, he was another who sadly perished in the Munich air disaster, at the age of just 28.

15 GARY NEVILLE

A true one-club man, right-back Gary Neville never played for any other team, with his career at Manchester United lasting from 1992 until 2011. Along with his brother Phil and players such as Ryan Giggs and Paul Scholes, he was part of Alex Ferguson's very youthful and highly successful 1990s team. He worked closely with David Beckham down the right wing, often contributing assists. In total, he won 20 winners' medals, including the league title eight times and the Champions League twice. After he retired from playing, Neville was an assistant manager for England and briefly managed Valencia. He is a media pundit and co-owner of Salford City.

14 DAVID BECKHAM

A genuine icon both within and beyond the footballing world, David Beckham did play for other clubs, notably LA Galaxy, but spent the majority of his career, from 1991 — he made his first-team debut in 1992 at age 17 — to 2003, at Manchester United. A creative midfielder known for his ability to pass accurately and bend free kicks, he was a consummate set-piece specialist. Alongside Ryan Giggs, Paul Scholes and the Neville brothers (with whom he co-owns Salford City), he was part of Alex Ferguson's extremely successful 1990s team and won multiple honours, making 394 appearances for the club and scoring 85 goals.

12 PETER SCHMEICHEL

A great Dane in every sense of the words, goalkeeper Peter Schmeichel is 1.93 metres (6'4") and weighed almost 100 kilos (15 st 10 lb) back in his playing days. In fact, he had to have XXXL football shirts made specially for him. Virtually unknown outside Denmark when Alex Ferguson bought him, he is widely recognised as one of the greatest goalkeepers in the world. He spent eight years — most of the 1990s — at United and captained the team in the 1999 Champions League final, the game which sealed the Treble and meant he was able to leave the club on an incredible high.

13 BRYAN ROBSON

The longest-serving captain in Manchester United history, Bryan Robson always led by example. Whether in attack or defence, he used his passing skills, pace and forcefulness creatively — and he never gave up. He made 461 appearances for the Red Devils, scoring 99 goals, many of them from late runs into the area. Brought to United by Ron Atkinson, for whom he played at West Bromwich Albion, he was a mainstay at Old Trafford for 13 years and won numerous honours, including two league titles, three FA Cups and a European Cup-Winners' Cup. Captain Marvel, as he is affectionately known, still works for the club, as a global ambassador.

11 ROY KEANE

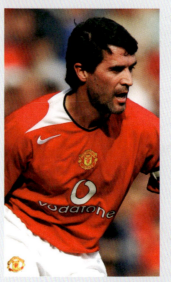

Born in Cork, Irishman Roy Keane arrived at Old Trafford in 1993 and quickly established himself as a first-choice midfielder. He led from the front and put fear into the opposition, and Alex Ferguson described him as the best midfielder he had ever worked with. As a result of Keane's criticism of people who claim to be interested in football but aren't, the term "prawn sandwich brigade" entered the language. In 12 years he made 480 appearances, scored 51 goals, and won 17 titles and trophies, and since retiring as a player has forged a successful career as a football pundit.

10 ▶ CRISTIANO RONALDO

Cristiano Ronaldo, who hails from the Portuguese island of Madeira, had two spells at Manchester United, the first more successful than the second. He initially came to Old Trafford in 2003 as a teenager and developed into a superb, highly skilful player, who, in addition to the honours he achieved with United, won the prestigious Ballon d'Or international award five times. In 2009 he left to go to Real Madrid and then Juventus, but returned to Manchester in 2021 when, after initially making a positive impact, his relationship with club and manager declined, and he left in 2022 to play in Saudi Arabia.

9 ▶ WAYNE ROONEY

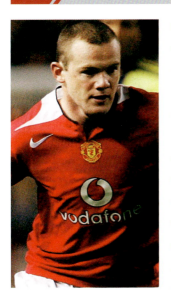

He arrived in 2004 from Everton, a teenager with a precocious talent, and stayed 13 years, during which time he won Premier League titles, League Cups, the FA Cup, Europa League and Champions League. Along the way he scored 253 goals for Manchester United and is the club's all-time leading scorer — he received the Golden Boot award from Bobby Charlton, the man whose record he surpassed. Although sometimes prone to injury and the occasional angry outburst, Wayne Rooney was a phenomenal player, comfortable both up front and in midfield, and his contribution to the club was outstanding.

8 ▶ MARCUS RASHFORD

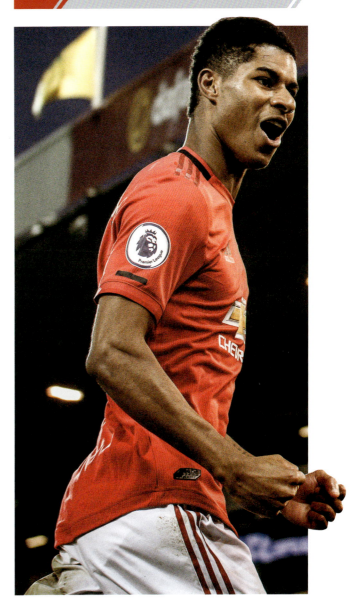

Manchester born and bred, Marcus Rashford's potential was spotted at an early age and he is very much a product of the youth system. He made his first-team (and simultaneously European) debut in February 2016, against a Danish side in a Europa League game, and he scored twice. Still only in his mid-twenties, he has won some silverware, but hasn't yet been part of a United golden era. He has, however, played for five different managers, so hopefully the stability the sixth, Erik ten Hag, has brought will mean a new golden era for United and for Rashford.

7 > PAUL SCHOLES

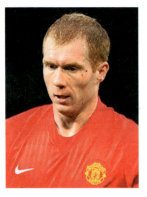

Although he didn't make his first-team debut until 1994, Paul Scholes was part of the Class of '92 and played a crucial role in the success of Alex Ferguson's Manchester United team throughout the 1990s, including the 1995-96 Double-winning and 1998-99 Treble-winning campaigns. Majestic in midfield, he was always an absolute pleasure to watch. He could conjure a way through to goal out of nowhere — in 718 appearances he scored 155 times — and his passes were accurate to the centimetre. He retired once, in 2011, but missed playing for the Red Devils so much he came back before retiring again in 2013.

5 > RYAN GIGGS

Ryan Giggs was a Manchester United player for 23 years, which is a long time to spend in any job. He was a member of the Class of '92, and part of the 1994 and 1996 Double-winning, and 1999 Treble-winning, sides. He made 963 appearances in all competitions, scoring 168 goals. However, his contribution to the club went way beyond goals. Although easily capable of stunning solo strikes, like his Treble year FA Cup semi-final goal against Arsenal, he also used his skill and sharp footballing brain on the pitch to lay on goals for his teammates.

6 > DENIS LAW

United fans called him the Lawman or the King, although to opposition fans he was Denis the Menace. Denis Law was an early football foreign export and in 1962 he was playing in Italy, for Turin, but, ever the visionary, Matt Busby brought him back to England, to Manchester United, where he stayed for over a decade. He entertained the crowds, he scored — he was versatile and there was no such thing as a typical Denis Law goal — and, although injury prevented him from playing in the 1968 European Cup, he was integral to that 1960s side and United through and through.

4 > DUNCAN EDWARDS

He made his first-team debut in 1953, at 16 years of age. However, five years later, although he initially survived the 1958 Munich air disaster, he tragically died in hospital two weeks after the crash of the injuries he had sustained in it. Busby Babe Duncan Edwards was a defensive midfielder with real class. A powerful presence on the pitch, he was adept at thwarting the opposition's attacking moves, picking up the ball and surging forward into dangerous positions. Extremely popular with supporters and colleagues alike, his career was cut short and who knows what he might have achieved had he lived.

3 ERIC CANTONA

In the popular imagination, the Frenchman is probably best remembered for his cryptic philosophical pronouncements and taking out a Crystal Palace supporter with a kung-fu kick, but Eric Cantona made so much more of an impact on Manchester United than that. It's true that he was no stranger to controversy, but in a relatively short space of time at the club, he achieved four league titles, including winning the Premier League title the first time it was contested, and two Doubles, scoring 82 goals in 182 appearances over five years, before his somewhat abrupt retirement in 1997.

2 BOBBY CHARLTON

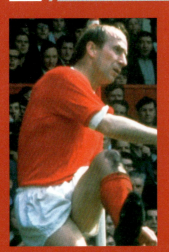

The great Bobby Charlton is without doubt an icon and, as a survivor of the Munich air disaster in 1958, something of a talisman for Manchester United. He was at the centre of the team Matt Busby rebuilt after the devastation of the crash and determinedly led the team to that magnificent victory in the European Cup ten years later, scoring twice in the final himself. He was a versatile player and over almost two decades with the club his contribution was enormous. For a long time he held United's appearances and goals records, until he was overtaken by Ryan Giggs and Wayne Rooney respectively.

1 GEORGE BEST

He famously asked that people should remember him for the back-page headlines, not the front-page ones, and it's true that George Best's story was ultimately dominated by the drinking, the womanising and the playboy lifestyle. However, the real story was about the Northern Irishman's ability on the ball, his skills, his speed, the way he could score from seemingly impossible positions. In short, he was a Manchester United legend due to his sheer footballing genius. He played for other clubs, but his 470 appearances and 179 goals in just over a decade prove that he was, at heart, a United man and is indisputably worthy of the number one spot.

TOP 5 GREATEST MANAGERS OF ALL TIME

The most successful have been incisive tacticians, skilful man-motivators and hard taskmasters, as well as fascinating characters in their own right. Much is expected of Manchester United managers, but the best have delivered trophies and titles to the delight of the Old Trafford faithful. Those managers have ensured the status of the club, cementing its popularity around the world, and their legacies will continue to be celebrated by generations of fans to come.

▶ The great men who have taken Manchester United to the top

TOP 5 GREATEST MANAGERS OF ALL TIME

107

ERNEST MANGNALL

A FIRM BELIEVER IN PHYSICAL FITNESS AND FOSTERING TEAM SPIRIT

The name Ernest Mangnall may not be as familiar to fans as those of Sir Matt Busby or Sir Alex Ferguson, but Mangnall was Manchester United's third highest-achieving manager ever and, just like his illustrious successors, took the club right to the top. Born in Bolton, Lancashire, in 1866, Mangnall was an amateur goalkeeper who later became a director of his local club, Bolton Wanderers. His first job in management, in 1890, was with Burnley, but in 1903 he was appointed as "secretary" — the term the club used at the time for manager — of Manchester United.

This was quite a surprise, given that his record at his two previous clubs was hardly glowing — both were relegated on his watch — and he didn't exactly have a reputation for encouraging his players to play beautiful, flowing football. He was, however, a firm believer in physical fitness and fostering team spirit, and club owner John Davies was prepared to give him the money to go out and build a strong squad, so he purchased several players, including centre-half Charlie Roberts from Grimsby for a record £600 transfer fee.

At the time, United were in the Second Division and that's where they stayed for his first two seasons of Mangnall's tenure, but at the third attempt they scored 90 goals in 38 games and, as runners-up to Bristol City in the 1905-06 season, achieved promotion to the First Division. The following year the FA investigated Manchester City and found they had been illegally paying their players more than the permitted maximum £4 a week. Consequently, in January 1907 City were forced to sell a number of players and Mangnall picked up the talented Billy Meredith for a mere £500, plus three others from the City squad.

Mangnall's Manchester United team attacked energetically, defended robustly and kicked off the 1907-08 season with three straight wins. They then lost to Middlesbrough 2-1, but followed that up with ten wins on the trot, which put them comfortably out in front in the title race. In late March they faltered again, losing to Liverpool 7-4, but they then charged towards the finish line and ended the season winning the First Division title by a healthy nine points. This would be the first of many such triumphs.

The following season, United went on a strong FA Cup run, passing Brighton & Hove Albion, Everton, Blackburn Rovers, Burnley and Newcastle United to face Bristol City in the Cup Final at the Crystal Palace ground. In the end it was a rather unremarkable game, but thanks to a Sandy Turnbull goal United won 1-0 to lift the famous trophy. Again, this would be the first of

IN THIS ERA UNITED WERE PLAYING AT A GROUND IN BANK STREET

many such triumphs.

In this era United were playing at a ground in Bank Street, in the suburb of Clayton, five kilometres east of the city centre. This had a capacity of 50,000, but it was decided that it wasn't grand enough for a team that had won the First Division and FA Cup, so John Davies paid £60,000 for a parcel of land in Old Trafford, thee kilometres southwest of the city, and commissioned Archibald Leitch, the most famous stadium architect of the day, to design a fitting home for the club, complete with tearooms and bars, and a gym, massage room and plunge baths for the players.

The construction budget was £30,000 and when it opened in February 1910 Old Trafford had a capacity of 77,000. The money may have been Davies's, but the vision was very much Mangnall's and he was determined that the team's on-pitch performance would prove worthy of such majestic surroundings.

On the last Saturday of the 1910-11 season, United were at home to Sunderland, second in the table and just a single point behind Aston Villa, whereas Villa were away to Liverpool. United won 5-1, but at the end of the game the crowd were quiet as they waited to hear the Anfield result. The tension was almost unbearable until a cheer suddenly went up and around the ground as news filtered through that Aston Villa had lost 3-1, so United were First Division champions for the second time.

Ernest Mangnall died in 1932, but is unique among managers in that he is the only one to have managed not just Manchester United, but Manchester City as well. It seems less likely to happen in the modern era, but after nine years at United, in 1912 he moved to manage City, where he clocked up 12 years and masterminded City's move to Maine Road, before retiring in 1924.

▼ Ernest Mangnall in 1908

Club Awards:
▶ First Division: 1907-08, 1910-11
▶ FA Cup: 1908-09
▶ FA Charity Shield: 1908, 1911

SIR MATT BUSBY

ONE OF THE GREATEST MANAGERS OF ALL TIME

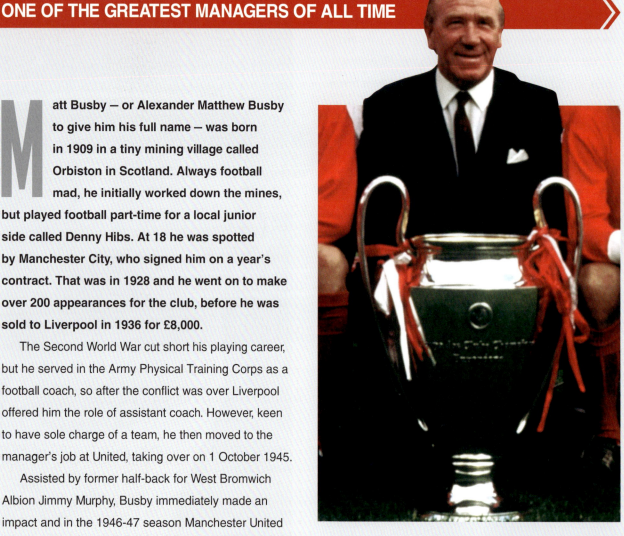

Matt Busby — or Alexander Matthew Busby to give him his full name — was born in 1909 in a tiny mining village called Orbiston in Scotland. Always football mad, he initially worked down the mines, but played football part-time for a local junior side called Denny Hibs. At 18 he was spotted by Manchester City, who signed him on a year's contract. That was in 1928 and he went on to make over 200 appearances for the club, before he was sold to Liverpool in 1936 for £8,000.

The Second World War cut short his playing career, but he served in the Army Physical Training Corps as a football coach, so after the conflict was over Liverpool offered him the role of assistant coach. However, keen to have sole charge of a team, he then moved to the manager's job at United, taking over on 1 October 1945.

Assisted by former half-back for West Bromwich Albion Jimmy Murphy, Busby immediately made an impact and in the 1946-47 season Manchester United claimed the First Division's runners-up spot, behind Liverpool. They then went on to achieve second place in the league in 1948, when they also won the FA Cup, 1949 and 1951, before they actually won the league in 1952. This was a fine run of achievements, but the team, captained by Johnny Carey, was beginning to age, so Busby set out to recruit a new set of players.

The manager could have gone out with a shopping list and splashed the cash, but instead he chose to replace the older players with youngsters of 16 and 17, among them, forward Billy Whelan, centre-half Bill Foulkes and left-half Duncan Edwards, widely held to be the best player of his generation. The few players he did buy from other clubs included forward Tommy

▶ Matt Busby on crutches, 18 April 1958

Taylor and keeper Harry Gregg. This was the team famously nicknamed the Busby Babes and they won the league in both 1956-57 and 1957-58, as well as being defeated by Aston Villa in the 1957 FA Cup Final.

When the 1957-58 season began Manchester United were on track for the treble of league title, FA Cup and European Cup, but on 6 February 1958, on the way back from a European Cup game against Red Star Belgrade, their plane crashed on the Munich Airport runway. Seven players and three club officials were among the 21 people who died at the scene. The final death toll was 23, with Duncan Edwards dying of his injuries two weeks later. Johnny Berry and Jackie Blanchflower were so badly injured they never played again and Busby himself received multiple injuries, was given the last rites twice (he was a staunch Catholic) and spent nine weeks in hospital, but he recovered.

Busby had rebuilt the team before and he rebuilt it again, basing it around survivors of the crash, Bill Foulkes, Harry Gregg and Bobby Charlton, and promoting players like Shay Brennan and Johnny Giles from the reserve and youth teams. He also signed new players, including Denis Law in 1962 and George Best in 1963 — and the strategy paid off.

Manchester United beat Leicester City 3-1 to lift the 1963 FA Cup and were league champions in both 1965 and 1967. They would have topped the First Division in 1968 too, had they not been pipped at the post by Manchester City on the last day of the season. However, the pinnacle of Busby's career as United manager took place on 29 May 1968, when, a decade after the Munich air crash, saw off two-times winners Benfica 4-1 in the final to win the European Cup.

When he retired a year later in 1969, with former

◀ In 1968 Busby realised his dream when United beat Benfica 4-1 at Wembley to win their first European Cup

player Wilf McGuinness appointed as his successor, he stayed on as a director of the club and when McGuinness was fired half-way through the following season he stepped in again as manager on an interim basis.

Generally regarded as one of the greatest managers of all time (and of any club), Matt Busby was a loyal servant to Manchester United — in the mid-1950s he was offered but declined the manager's job at Real Madrid. In addition to the many honours he won over the course of 25 distinguished years, he was the first manager of an English team to win the European Cup and was subsequently awarded a knighthood in recognition of that fact. He died in 1994 at the age of 84.

Personal Awards:
▶ PFA Merit Award: 1980
▶ English Football Hall of Fame (Manager): 2002
▶ European Hall of Fame (Manager): 2008

Club Awards:
▶ First Division: 1951-52, 1955-56, 1956-57, 1964-65, 1966-67
▶ FA Cup: 1947-48, 1962-63
▶ FA Charity Shield: 1952, 1956, 1957, 1965 (shared), 1967 (shared)
▶ European Cup: 1967-68

TOMMY DOCHERTY

INSTRUMENTAL IN UNITED'S REJUVENATION AFTER THE GOLDEN YEARS

Tommy Docherty was born in Glasgow in 1928. He played as a hard-tackling right-half for several teams, starting with Celtic, which was the first professional club to sign him, in 1947. This was followed by Preston North End, for whom he made 324 appearances; Arsenal; and, briefly, Chelsea. He was also capped 25 times for Scotland's national side. He then went on to become a manager and between 1961 and 1988 he managed a total of 13 clubs, including, from 1972 to 1977, Manchester United.

When he pitched up at Old Trafford, the triumphs of the Busby years were long gone and the club had been struggling to find a manager who could emulate that level of success. Tommy Docherty, often known simply as the Doc, was that man. His arrival mid-way through the 1972-73 season gave the team the bounce it needed to swerve relegation, albeit only just.

At this point United stalwarts Bobby Charlton and Denis Law left the club, followed a short while later by George Best, but the Doc brought in some new faces, including classy midfielder Lou Macari, whom he bought from Celtic right under the noses of Liverpool who were poised to sign him, popular defender Jim Holton from Shrewsbury Town and forward Stuart Pearson from Hull City.

United weren't able to avoid the drop for ever, though, and a year later, having won a mere ten games and lost 20 in the 1973-74 season, they found themselves in 21st place and out of the First Division for the first time in nigh on 40 years. However, they didn't languish in League Two for long, shooting straight back up to the First Division the following season and playing some of the most attractive football the red side of Manchester had seen for some time.

Back in the top flight in 1975-76 they were unbeaten at home for the entire season. In the final game they saw off City 2-0 with goals from Gordon Hill and Sammy McIlroy to achieve an impressive third position, which meant they qualified for the following season's UEFA Cup. They also went to Wembley for that season's Cup Final. Granted, they were beaten 1-0 by Southampton, but Docherty had nonetheless proved that the United directors were right to keep faith with him. He also told anyone who would listen that they'd be back for the trophy next year.

True to his word, the day of the 1977 FA Cup Final dawned and in front of a Wembley crowd of over 99,000 United were set to face a Liverpool side managed by Bob Paisley, having seen off Walsall, Queens Park Rangers, Southampton (but only after a replay), Aston Villa and Leeds United. It remained 0-0 until half-time, but early in the second half, in the space of about five minutes, there was a flurry of goals.

First Stuart Pearson opened the account for United, picking up a long ball and shooting past Ray Clemence, the Liverpool keeper. Two minutes later Jimmy Case equalised for Liverpool with a half-volley into the top of the net that Alex Stepney just couldn't get to. Then three minutes after that Lou Macari's shot was deflected off the chest of his teammate Jimmy Greenhoff and into the goal, past Clemence and Phil Neal, who was standing on the line. It was 2-1 to Manchester United and that's how it stayed. They had vanquished Liverpool and won the FA Cup, depriving the Merseysiders of the chance to win the treble in the process.

That was undoubtedly the high point of Docherty's stay at the club. The low point came very shortly afterwards, when it was revealed that Docherty, who had been married to his wife Agnes for almost 30 years, was having an affair with Mary Brown, wife of the club's physiotherapist Laurie Brown. The board sacked him, citing gross misconduct, and the Doc's reign at United

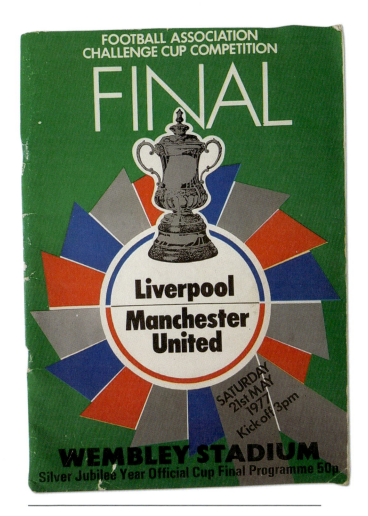

▲ 1977 FA Cup Final programme

◄ Tommy Docherty signing photos as Chelsea manager in 1962

was over, although he did eventually marry Mary.

Often described as outspoken or controversial, and always a larger-than-life character, Tommy Docherty wasn't the longest-lived United manager, nor was he identified solely with Manchester United — fans of Chelsea, Derby or even the Scottish national team could legitimately claim him as their own — but he was instrumental in United's rejuvenation after the golden years of the Matt Busby era had faded into memory and he undoubtedly left an indelible mark on the club's history.

Club Awards:
- Second Division: 1974-75
- FA Cup: 1976-77

RON ATKINSON

ALWAYS FOCUSED ON GETTING THE BEST OUT OF HIS PLAYERS

Ronald Atkinson, often known as Big Ron, was born in 1939 in Liverpool and grew up outside Birmingham. His first job was as a groundsman at Wolverhampton Wanderers, but he signed to Aston Villa at 17, although he never made a first-team appearance for them. He then moved to Oxford United (called Headington United at the time) and played over 500 games there as a wing-half, captaining the side as they rose from the Southern League, through the divisions, to reach Division Two in just six years, in 1968. He retired from playing three years later at the age of 32 and went into management.

Over ten years he managed non-league Kettering United, Fourth Division Cambridge United, who he took to the Second Division, and First Division West Bromwich Albion. He did very well at West Brom; well enough to be offered the Manchester United job and in 1981 he took over from a sacked Dave Sexton.

The club hadn't won any silverware for four years, so everyone was hopeful Atkinson would inject some life back into the side. In 1981-82, his first season in charge, he bought midfielder Bryan Robson from West Brom for a British record of £1.5 million. He also brought in another midfielder from West Brom, Remi Moses, and Arsenal striker Frank Stapleton. United finished third in the league, which ensured they qualified for the UEFA Cup, and at the tail end of the season, away to Brighton and Hove Albion, Atkinson brought on a young sub called Norman Whiteside, who was just shy of his 17th birthday.

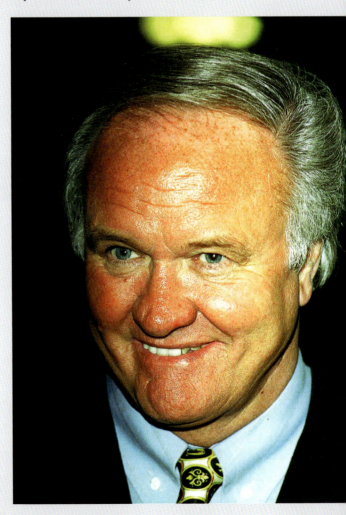

The following season, 1982-83, saw Whiteside make a real impact and United challenged for the league title, going top more than once. However, the previous champions, Liverpool, prevailed again, while United achieved third place again. In the FA Cup, they made two trips to Wembley to play Brighton and Hove Albion. The first ended in a 2-2 draw, the second in a 4-0 win for United. The Atkinson plan was working just as the board of directors and fans had hoped it would.

Unfortunately, when it came to defending their FA Cup holders' title, United crashed out of the competition very early on after a shock 2-0 defeat at the hands of Third Division Bournemouth. In the 1983-84 league it was a similar pattern to previous seasons: the team went top, but couldn't quite sustain it, this time finishing fourth.

Big Ron's problem was too many injuries to vital players and consequently too many draws, but the club did well in the European Cup-Winners' Cup. In the third round they met a Barcelona side featuring Maradona, losing the away leg 2-0, but managing an impressive 3-0 win at Old Trafford. That put them through to the semi-finals where they lost to Juventus.

At the end of the season midfielder Ray Wilkins was sold to AC Milan for the princely sum of £1.5 million, but at the same time a young striker called Mark Hughes had started to break through. Atkinson could have bought a player to fill Wilkins's boots, but instead he moved Whiteside into midfield and partnered Hughes up front with the experienced Stapleton.

United achieved another fourth league place in 1984-85, but were unable to take part in the European Cup-Winners' Cup due to the post-Heysel ban on English clubs competing in Europe. However, the FA Cup was theirs again when they beat Everton 1-0, the goal was scored by Whiteside in extra time. The game was also notable because United's Kevin Moran was

◄ 'Big Ron' was an easy-going, extroverted character

▲ Atkinson's United team celebrate their FA Cup final replay victory, 28 May 1983

the first player to be sent off in an FA Cup Final.

There was a strong sense of déjà vu about 1985-86: fourth place in the league yet again and still no European action, but no FA Cup win either and Bryan Robson was injured for half the season. There was also fan disappointment when Mark Hughes was sold to Barcelona. The 1986-87 season started with three defeats in a row and although there were some signs of improvement as the autumn progressed, by early November the board had had enough and Atkinson was fired.

Always focused on getting the best out of his players, he went on to manage several other clubs and had a high-profile career as a TV pundit in the 1990s and early 2000s, although he resigned from his role at ITV in 2004, after making a racist comment when he thought the microphone was turned off. However, in a five-year period at United he achieved five consecutive top four league finishes and two FA Cup triumphs, making him the club's most successful manager since Matt Busby.

Club Awards:
▶ FA Cup: 1982-83, 1984-85
▶ FA Charity Shield: 1983

SIR ALEX FERGUSON

IN TOTAL HIS MANCHESTER UNITED TEAMS WON 38 HONOURS

Sir Alex Ferguson managed Manchester United for 27 years, from 1986 to 2013. To stay in any job that long is impressive, but to achieve what Ferguson did in that time is extraordinary. Born in Glasgow in 1941, he played for several Scottish clubs before moving into management, eventually at Aberdeen, where he won a raft of honours, including the 1983 European Cup-Winners' Cup and the Scottish national team.

When he arrived in November 1986, they were 21st in the league, but he instilled discipline, results steadily improved and they finished the season in a respectable 11th place. The following season, 1987-88, boosted by new signings Steve Bruce and Brian McClair, they achieved second place (Liverpool won with a nine-point lead), but in 1988-89 they were back in 11th place.

Although Ferguson bought players like Paul Ince and Gary Pallister, 1989-90 looked like it would be even worse. They hovered above the relegation zone, eventually finishing 13th, and there were calls for Fergie to go. However, an FA Cup run saved him. They played Crystal Palace in the final. That ended 3-3, but thanks to defender Lee Martin United won the replay 1-0.

This was a turning point, but 1990-91 was still an uneven season. The team placed sixth, although a 17-year-old Ryan Giggs made his debut in a home defeat to Everton. They were runners-up to Sheffield Wednesday in the League Cup, though, and won the European Cup-Winners' Cup, beating Barcelona 2-1.

In 1991-92, they won the League Cup and European Super Cup, but lost the league to Leeds. However, in 1992-93 Ferguson signed Eric Cantona and by April they were comfortably second and moved up to first with a crucial win over Sheffield Wednesday, ending the season with a ten-point advantage over Aston Villa. Ferguson had finally won the league title — and the first Premier League title, too.

He bettered that in 1993-94 by winning not just the league, but beating Chelsea 4-0 in the FA Cup Final as well, making it a Double year. The following season, 1994-95, didn't go quite so smoothly, though. Cantona was banned for eight months for assaulting a Crystal Palace fan, they lost the title race by drawing 1-1 with West Ham in the final game and Everton defeated them 1-0 in the FA Cup Final.

Ince and Hughes left in summer 1995, but Ferguson made no new signings, because he believed he had a group of youngsters — David Beckham, Nicky Butt, Gary Neville, Phil Neville, Paul Scholes — who were ready to step up. He was right and former Liverpool player Alan Hansen, who famously said you can't win anything with kids, was wrong. United did the Double again, clinching it against Middlesbrough on the season's final day and triumphing 1-0 over Liverpool to take the FA Cup.

▶ Ferguson celebrates his 1,000th league game with United and announces his retirement, 2 September 2012

They went on to win their fourth league title in five attempts at the end of 1996-97, but in 1997-98, in a rare slip-up in this era, they came second. That was followed by three consecutive first places and then another minor hiccup with third place in 2002, before they achieved pole position again in 2002-03.

In 2003-04 United came third once more, but lifted the FA Cup instead after beating Millwall 3-0 thanks to a Cristiano Ronaldo header and two from Ruud van Nistelrooy. They were runners-up in the FA Cup the season after that — Arsenal won 5-4 on penalties — and it was a repeat third position in the 2004-05 league. They bettered that by one in 2005-06, finishing second, with winning the League Cup as some consolation.

The 2006-07 season was the start of another winning streak, with league-winning placings in that campaign and then four out of the next six. Even in the years when they missed the top spot — 2010 and 2012 — they were runners-up.

All this time, of course, United had been pursuing glory in Europe and in 1999 the seasons of effort finally paid off when — after a 31-year interval — they bested Bayern Munich 2-1 in an epic game to win the Champions League. They did it again almost ten years later, in 2008, when they met Chelsea in the final and won 6-5 on penalties.

Ferguson could be spiky and he always demanded total commitment, but his record speaks for itself. The list of impact players he developed or signed is long — future manager Ole Gunnar Solskjær, Peter Schmeichel, Roy Keane, Teddy Sheringham, Jaap Stam, Wayne Rooney — and in total his Manchester United teams won 38 honours, including 13 league titles, five FA Cups and two Champions Leagues. The great man was knighted in 1999 and retired in 2013, although he remains a director of the club.

Personal Awards:
▶ LMA Manager of the Decade: 1990s
▶ LMA Manager of the Year: 1992-93, 1998-99, 2007-08, 2010-11, 2012-13
▶ LMA Special Merit Award: 2009, 2011
▶ Premier League Manager of the Season: 1993-94, 1995-96, 1996-97, 1998-99, 1999-2000, 2002-03, 2006-07, 2007-08, 2008-09, 2010-11, 2012-13
▶ UEFA Manager of the Year: 1998-99
▶ BBC Sports Personality of the Year Coach Award: 1999
▶ World Soccer Magazine World Manager of the Year: 1993, 1999, 2007, 2008
▶ World Soccer Greatest Manager of All Time: 2013

Club Awards:
▶ Premier League: 1992-93, 1993-94, 1995-96, 1996-97, 1998-99, 1999-2000, 2000-01, 2002-03, 2006-07, 2007-08, 2008-09, 2010-11, 2012-13
▶ FA Cup: 1989-90, 1993-94, 1995-96, 1998-99, 2003-04
▶ League Cup: 1991-92, 2005-06, 2008-09, 2009-10
▶ FA Charity/Community Shield: 1990 (shared), 1993, 1994, 1996, 1997, 2003, 2007, 2008, 2010, 2011
▶ UEFA Champions League: 1998-99, 2007-08
▶ European Cup Winners' Cup: 1990-91
▶ European Super Cup: 1991
▶ Intercontinental Cup: 1999
▶ FIFA Club World Cup: 2008

TOP 10 GREATEST TEAMS OF ALL TIME

The Manchester United story is full of teams who have brought silverware and great acclaim to Old Trafford. They have captivated millions with their skills, passion and achievements. From the Red Devils' first league winners in 1908 to the Busby Babes to Alex Ferguson's all-conquering heroes, United have produced winners with style and steel. Definitively comparing teams from different times is an impossible task, but these ten have undoubtedly provided the glory and entertainment to secure their place in the club's history.

▶ The Busby Babes team pictured before the Munich air disaster, 8 February 1958 and Fergie's treble winners, 1999

TOP 10 GREATEST TEAMS OF ALL TIME

DOC'S DEVILS (1975-77)

▲ Manchester United are crowned Second Division champions after thrashing Blackpool 4-0 in the final match of the season, Old Trafford, 26 April 1975

Maybe it took relegation to the Second Division to give Tommy Docherty the time and space to build the kind of Manchester United team he wanted. With Charlton, Best and Law all having departed, goalkeeper Alex Stepney, now in his thirties, was the only survivor of the Busby era. He was at the base of an experienced spine in the team, which also featured club captain and centre-back Martin Buchan, the skilful Lou Macari and the ever-reliable Stuart Pearson up front. Around them were a team of youngsters, hopefuls brought in to the club, such as Steve Coppell and Gordon Hill, or promoted from within, like Arthur Albiston and Sammy McIlroy.

The team was industrious and tough. The midfield harried opponents, while Jim Holton, Jimmy Nicholl or Stewart Houston never shied away from a crunching tackle. Meanwhile, Docherty brought back the attractive football that was synonymous with the club. Alongside Macari, McIlroy and then Jimmy Greenhoff provided the flair, but it was the exciting wing paring of Coppell and Hill that got the crowd on their feet.

The team romped to the Second Division Championship in 1975 and looked like repeating the feat in the First Division the following season. They fell short, finished third and lost the FA Cup Final to Southampton, but Docherty kept faith with his young guns.

They were young (with an average age comparable to Fergie's Class of '92 when they were initially called up) and played with such dynamism, verve and spirit that they caught the public imagination. The 1976-77 season saw them finish as the league's second highest scorers, but only four teams conceded more. They ended up sixth and despite beating Ajax and Juventus at Old Trafford went out to the latter in the UEFA Cup.

The FA Cup salvaged the season as they dispensed with QPR, Aston Villa and Leeds en route to a final against Liverpool. There, goals from Stuart Pearson and Jimmy Greenhoff helped end a nine-year trophy drought (and denied Liverpool a Treble). There was good reason to be optimistic, but after Docherty's shock departure in the close season, the team that had brought a smile to English football and hope back to Manchester United never fulfilled their potential.

COMEBACK KINGS (2002-03)

▲ The Manchester United players and coaching staff celebrate being crowned Barclaycard Premiership Champions 2002-03 at the Carrington Training Ground on 5 May 2003

Manchester United's third place in the 2001-02 table had been a disappointment. Double-winning Arsenal manager was declaring it was now the London club's time to dominate and questions were being asked of Alex Ferguson. He acted decisively by making Rio Ferdinand the most expensive British player ever when he signed the defender for £30 million.

As in the previous year, the Red Devils struggled to find consistency through the early months of the season as injuries to Beckham, Ferdinand, Keane, Butt and Blanc disrupted the team. Beating Liverpool 2-1 at Anfield and Arsenal 2-0 at Old Trafford in successive games in early December put them back in the running, but after a Boxing Day defeat at Middlesbrough they were in third place, still trailing the Gunners by seven points.

It was a 2-0 victory over Birmingham City capped by a sublime chipped goal from Beckham that marked the turning point. The Reds would not lose a game for the rest of the season. Ahead of the often brilliant but mistake-prone Barthez in goal, Mikaël Silvestre's move to central defence alongside Ferdinand shored up a back four that included an increasingly assured Wes Brown, Gary Neville and the versatile John O'Shea. Nicky Butt replaced the injured Veron in midfield, Diego Forlan scored some vital goals, including a last-minute winner against Chelsea, and Ole Gunnar Solskjær proved an able replacement for an injured Beckham, notching up 15 league goals in the season.

In the chase for the title, Ruud Van Nistelrooy was unstoppable as Beckham, Giggs and Solskjær repeatedly picked him out. He scored in each of the final eight games of the season and picked up the Golden Boot. Alongside him Paul Scholes, playing in an advanced role, was superb. A highlight was his hat-trick in a 6-2 victory at Newcastle that sent United to the top for the first time. A 2-2 draw at Arsenal and four season-concluding victories saw them win the league with ease and said everything for Alex Ferguson: write us off at your peril.

GOAL-HUNGRY CHAMPIONS (1999-2000)

▲ Andy Cole, Dwight Yorke and Ryan Giggs of Manchester United in action, 2000

The best team Manchester United had ever had — that was the judgement of Alex Ferguson in 2000 after United had won the Premier League title for the sixth time in eight seasons. They scored 97 league goals that season and won the league by 18 points, a record that would stand for another 17 years. It was a season only overshowed by a surprise defeat by Real Madrid in the Champions League and United's controversial withdrawal from the FA Cup — a decision that might have cost them the Double.

United were still riding high from their Treble-winning season, but the team had one major change. Captain and goalkeeper Peter Schmeichel had moved on at the end of the previous season. His replacement, Mark Bosnich, did not convince, but the team still began the season with a nine-game unbeaten streak, including a 5-1 thrashing of Newcastle United with Andrew Cole a four-goal hero. However, when Bosnich was injured, new signing Massimo Taibi made a series of costly blunders, culminating in a 5-0 drubbing at Chelsea, which ended an undefeated run of 29 games.

Veteran keeper Raimond van der Gouw steadied the ship and from the end of October United embarked on another long unbeaten run. They reclaimed the top spot at the end of January and never relinquished control of the title race, suffering just one defeat in the rest of the season. Some of their victories were emphatic, too, such as a 5-1 win against Everton in which Solskjær scored four or a 7-1 pummelling of West Ham that featured a Paul Scholes hat-trick. In the last nine games, they amassed 32 goals as they strolled home, claiming the title with four games still to play.

This was a team at the peak of its powers. The defence of Jaap Stam and Mikaël Silvestre with the Neville brothers or Denis Irwin in the full-back roles were often broached, but that can be attributed to the attacking nature of the team. Dwight Yorke top-scored with 20 league goals, Andrew Cole registered 19 and Solskjær claimed 12 as a midfield of Scholes, Beckham, Giggs and the Professional Footballers' Association Players' Player of the Year and Football Writers' Association Footballer of the Year, Roy Keane, were all happy to push forward in a side which scored goals for fun.

THE AWARD-WINNERS (2006-07)

United had endured a three-year Premier title drought having been overshadowed by Arsenal and then Chelsea, but a 14-game run-in with just one defeat to the Champions-elect at the close of the 2005-06 campaign gave them hope for the following season. Tottenham's elegant passer Michael Carrick was the only major incomer at close season, an impressive if not like-for-like replacement for the soon-to-be-departed Roy Keane.

How Ferguson could match high-speeding and high-achieving Chelsea, and how the Rooney-Ronaldo World Cup spat and the absence of van Nistelrooy, now at Real Madrid, would affect goalscoring were the big pre-season questions and both were answered emphatically. Apart from one week in September, United topped the league all season, while the two Rs scored 23 goals apiece in all competitions.

Goalkeeper Van der Saar provided a reassuring presence, while Patrice Evra, Gabriel Heinze and Nemanja Vidić bolstered the familiar defensive line. In midfield, South Korean Park Ji-Song and Scot Darren Fletcher aided Scholes, Carrick and Giggs, while for strikers it was a free-for-all with the often-injured Louis Saha, on-loan Henrik Larsson and Ole Gunnar Solskjær in his last season all adding to Rooney and Ronaldo's fire-power. Notable games included a 5-1 thrashing of Fulham in the opening game, a Wayne Rooney hat-trick

▲ Ferguson congratulates Alan Smith as they celebrate winning the Premiership title at the end of the match against West Ham at Old Trafford, 13 May 2007

in a 4-0 victory at Bolton, John O'Shea's 92nd-minute winner at Anfield and a Ronaldo masterclass as United despatched Aston Villa 3-0 at Villa Park.

The Red Devils were also marching on in two cup competitions. A Champions League run included an impressive defeat of Benfica and an unforgettable 7-1 demolition of Roma, but sadly they came unstuck in the semi-final against AC Milan. Meanwhile, they strolled to the first FA Cup Final at the new Wembley, only for Drogba's extra-time strike to decide an uninspiring match. It was a matter of "what could have been" for a team in their pomp.

Just how good this team was is illustrated by the end-of-season awards they picked up. Eight members of the squad (Van der Sar, Neville, Ferdinand, Vidić, Evra, Scholes, Giggs and Ronaldo) made it into the Premier League team of the season, Sir Alex Ferguson was presented with the Manager of the Season award and Cristiano Ronaldo collected the Football Writers' Association's Footballer of the Year, the Professional Footballers' Association's equivalent and its Young Player of the Year.

OLD HANDS AND YOUNG GUNS (1995-96)

▲ Open-top bus parade through Manchester after winning the FA Cup and Premiership Double, May 1996

The words of Match of the Day pundit Alan Hansen after United's opening day defeat by Aston Villa — that you'll never win anything with kids — are now part of football folklore. After the Red Devils' first trophyless season of the 1990s, they had sold key players Paul Ince, Mark Hughes and Andrei Kanchelskis and, instead of spending millions like their rivals, replaced them with promising young players from within the club's ranks.

David Beckham, Nicky Butt, Paul Scholes, Ryan Giggs, Gary Neville and Phil Neville — they were all under 22 and they were given the responsibility to help put United back at the top of the pile. They had the talent, had won the FA Youth Cup and were among the gems of the England Youth and Under-21 teams. They did not disappoint, quickly coming of age in a season where United became the first ever team to do the League and FA Cup Double twice.

Despite winning the next five matches, results remained patchy until the New Year. It was the experienced and very capable old heads — Steve Bruce, Gary Pallister, Denis Irwin, Brian McClair and the imperious Peter Schmeichel in goal — who helped them through a difficult period. They were aided by Roy Keane, the "old" head in midfield, striker Andrew Cole in his first full season at Old Trafford, a resurgent Lee Sharpe and the returning King Eric.

Cantona came back from his long suspension in October, but it wasn't until the New Year that he began to exert his influence. He scored in six consecutive league games and in four of those he got the only goal of the match, including the decider against title rivals Newcastle and a 25-metre half-volley against Arsenal in March which took United to the top of the league.

The last month of the season was tense with Newcastle breathing down United's neck, but they held firm, clinching the league title by beating Middlesbrough in the last game of the season. A week later they were in the FA Cup Final. A Cantona-inspired run and a semi-final comeback, sealed by a Beckham winner against Chelsea, set up a final against Liverpool. The game itself wasn't particularly memorable, but it was Eric Cantona who secured the Double just five minutes from full-time.

MEAN AND MAGNIFICENT (2008-09)

If United were suffering a hangover as Champions of Europe, it didn't last long. After a month they were 15th in the league, but they ended the season completing a hat-trick of consecutive Premier League titles, won the League Cup, became the first English club to be crowned Champions of the World and reached the Champions League final again.

It wasn't the most scintillating United team ever, but it was one of the most effective. It was built on a defence marshalled by Nemanja Vidić at his peak, with O'Shea, Ferdinand, Evans and Rafael all playing to a consistently high standard. They enabled United to keep 23 clean sheets in the league and Edwin van der Sar to set a new record of 1311 minutes without conceding. Midfield was compact with Ryan Giggs reverting to the centre alongside Carrick and Anderson, Fletcher or Paul Scholes, who had made his 600th United appearance by the season's end. The attacking line-up had been strengthened with the signing of Dimitar Berbatov from Spurs, but Ronaldo and Rooney supplied most of the goals with Berbatov, Park Ji-Song, Carlos Tevez, Giggs, Nani and Cantona chipping in.

United were still third as the year ended, but a run of 14 consecutive clean sheets landed them in pole position. They went top with a 1-0 win at Bolton Wanderers courtesy of a Berbatov 90th-minute header. Last-gasp winners were to be a feature of the season. After a mid-March hiccup including a nightmare 4-1 thrashing by Liverpool at Old Trafford, it was a 93rd-minute winner against Aston Villa by 17-year-old Italian Federico Macheda which put them back on track and a late winner by Michael Carrick against Wigan that set them up for the title with two games to go.

United had already won the League Cup on penalties against Tottenham, but it was retaining the

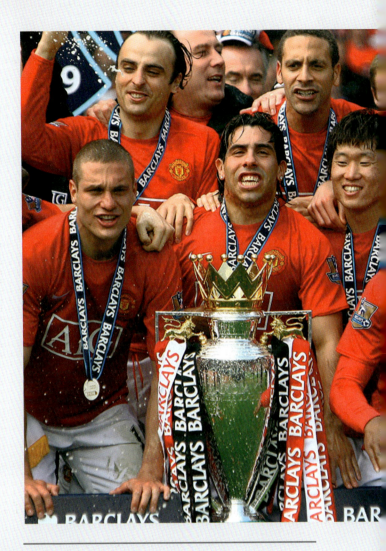

▲ Manchester United celebrate after winning the Premier League, 2009

Champions League that was utmost in fans' minds. That seemed possible after they dispatched Arsenal 3-1 in the semi-final second leg. The performance displayed the team's characteristic resilience, power and energy at its ruthless best. It included a 40-metre swerving free kick by Ronaldo and the same player finishing off a lightning counter-attack. However, in the final in the stifling Rome, a Barcelona team inspired by Iniesta, Xavi and Messi proved just too good.

THE BUSBY BABES (1955-58)

▲ The team pictured before the Munich air disaster, 8 February 1958

After his team had won the 1951-52 league title, Matt Busby had begun to rebuild. Rather than sign players from other clubs, he looked to his young players who, under soon-to-be assistant manager Jimmy Murphy, won the first five FA Youth Cups. The team he created would be remembered forever, not just by United fans, but by football fans the world over.

The average age of the side which won the Championship in 1955-56 was just 22, the youngest ever title-winning team. They were playing free-flowing attacking football and neutrals up and down the land flocked to see them. The majestic Duncan Edwards, still only 21 but with 18 England caps to his name, was paired at half-back with Eddie Colman, 20, who had broken into the team that season along with Bobby Charlton, 19, at inside-left. The young players were "chaperoned" by a spine of more experienced players: captain Roger Byrne, a full-back who loved to attack; goalkeeper Ray Wood; centre-half Bill Foulkes; diminutive winger Johnny Berry and centre-forward Tommy Taylor, who was dominant in the air and a great goalscorer.

The following season, 1956-57, United won the title for the second year, amassing 103 league goals.

Tommy Taylor, 21-year-old Irish international Billy Whelan, and inside-forwards Bobby Charlton and Dennis Viollet all reached double figures. The Red Devils might even have secured the elusive Double if fate hadn't been cruel. After just six minutes in the FA Cup Final against Aston Villa, keeper Ray Wood broke his jaw after a (then legal) shoulder barge. He was replaced by an outfield player and, with the team effectively down to ten men, United lost 2-1.

Busby had bigger ambitions for his young team. In 1956 they became the first English team to enter the European Cup. They progressed to the semi-final, beating Anderlect 10-0 and overcoming a 5-3 deficit against Athletic Bilbao. However, in the semi-final Real Madrid, the Kings of Europe, secured a 3-1 home win and United could only draw the home leg 2-2. Matt Busby described the pre-Munich team as potentially the best club side he had ever seen and no one doubted that, had tragedy not intervened, this gifted team would have become even stronger.

KINGS OF EUROPE (1967-68)

A decade on from the tragedy which broke the heart of the club, Manchester United became European champions for the first time. With Bill Foulkes and Bobby Charlton the only survivors still in the team, Busby had assembled a new team that, if unassuming with a defence of Burns, Foulkes, Sadler and Dunne, had steel in a midfield of Paddy Crerand and Nobby Stiles, and flair to spare in an attack that featured Charlton, Best, Law and youngsters Brian Kidd and John Aston.

As champions, United were favourites to win the league, but a slow start and too many draws meant they couldn't seem to shake off a chasing pack of Manchester City, Liverpool and Leeds United, although they scored freely, with George Best enjoying a breakout season with 28 goals, Charlton scoring 20, Kidd 17, Law 11 and Aston 10.

United were particularly deadly at home, where they posted four without reply against Coventry, Wolves and Fulham, and thrashed Newcastle 6-0 on the penultimate game of the season, with Best registering his first hat-trick. In the final game, they needed to win and City had to drop points at Newcastle. Neither happened and United had to settle for the runners-up spot.

Four days later, though, they were at the Bernabeu defending a slim 1-0 first leg advantage over Real Madrid after the first leg of the semi-final. They had progressed through the competition reasonably comfortably, having conceded two goals in their six games against Hibernian, FK Sarajevo and Górnik Zabrze, but Real were a different proposition. They wiped out the deficit after half an hour and by half-time were leading 3-2 on aggregate and very much in control.

However, in a second-half thriller, United took the game to the Spanish giants. The defenders grabbed the headlines as Sadler levelled the tie and with just ten minutes remaining Foulkes turned in a Best pull-back to send United to the final. When United met Benfica at Wembley it was another of the great games of English football. Stepney kept the English side in the game after the Portuguese team equalised Charlton's flicked header with ten minutes left, but three goals in seven extra-time minutes blew Eusebio's team away.

▲ United's John Aston in an aerial duel with Adolfo of Benfica in the European Cup Final at Wembley, 29 May 1968.

DOUBLE CHAMPIONS (2007-08)

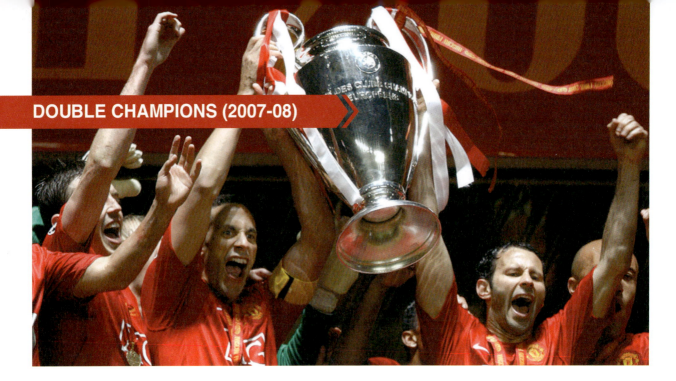

▲ United celebrate with the Champions League trophy after victory over Chelsea, Moscow 2008

Staying ahead of Chelsea, Arsenal and Liverpool was no mean feat. It took a team of defensive fortitude and attacking prowess, who would cap their domestic success by becoming European Champions again. However, despite strengthening his title-winning team with Owen Hargreaves, Nani, Anderson and Carlos Tevez, an injury-hit forward line soon left United playing catch-up in the league. Eight straight wins helped as Ferguson's shift to a 4-3-3 began to bear fruit with striking trio Rooney, Ronaldo and Tevez combining to terrorise defences.

The forward line, aided by Scholes, Park Ji-Song and Giggs, was sharp, but the defensive unit was almost impenetrable. In front of van der Saar, Ferdinand and Vidić were a perfect central combination, full-backs Evra and Brown had fabulous seasons and Hargreaves patrolled magnificently. They conceded just seven league goals at Old Trafford all season.

United were in fine form in the New Year, putting 11 past Newcastle in two games and outclassing Liverpool in a 3-0 victory at Old Trafford, but so were their London rivals. Arsenal collapsed after a virtuoso Rooney display resulted in a 4-0 FA Cup thrashing, but defeat at Chelsea left United having to beat Wigan on the last day of the season to retain the trophy. Fittingly, the 2-0 win was sealed by Ryan Giggs, who equalled Bobby Charlton's record of 758 appearances.

In the Champions League United had sailed through the group stage and the knockout games against Lyon and Roma, conceding just five goals in ten games, but they faced a tough semi-final against Barcelona. Having held firm for a 0-0 draw in Spain, Paul Scholes' spectacular rising 25-metre drive settled the tie in Manchester.

In a thrilling final in Moscow, United and Chelsea traded blows with Cristiano Ronaldo (soon to win his first Ballon d'Or), the key player for the Manchester side. He rose above the defence to head United ahead, his 42nd goal of the season. However the sides went in equal at half-time, full-time and extra-time. After Ronaldo missed the third kick of the penalty shootout, United looked like missing out, but John Terry's slip in the crucial penalty and Van der Saar's save from Anelka in sudden death turned things around. On the 50th anniversary of the Munich air crash, Manchester United's victory was as poignant as it was euphoric.

TREBLE TOP (1998-99)

▲ Alex Ferguson is held aloft by his team as they celebrate victory in the Champions League Final against Bayern Munich at the Nou Camp Stadium in Barcelona, 1999

▼ Manchester United celebrate winning the FA Premier League title after their victory over Tottenham, 16 May 1999

It was a season forged by passion, skill and a little luck, where United's home-grown players excelled, where Jaap Stam and Dwight Yorke proved to be perfect signings and the whole squad played their part. They only lost three times in the league, remained unbeaten in the Champions League, scored some fantastic goals and won all three major trophies. It was historic.

With the return of Roy Keane from injury, the team looked solid, skilful and full of goals. Schmeichel and Stam calmly led the defence, and in midfield Beckham, Giggs and Scholes were no longer promising talent but special players. And when Yorke's partnership with Cole clicked, they were unstoppable. Early hopes of regaining the title, however, were dented as defensive frailties and wasteful draws left United languishing in fourth place at Christmas. With a new year came a new United, though, and the sparks of the Yorke-Cole partnership turned into raging fires which saw Leicester City beaten 6-2 and Nottingham Forest 8-1 at their own stadiums. United would not lose again this season — in any competition.

By April, the Reds were top of the league, two points clear of Arsenal. Then the magic began. A mesmerising FA Cup semi-final replay against Arsenal was won by a ten-men United through an extra-time Ryan Giggs wonder goal. Giggs had also been the hero the week before with an injury time equaliser against Juventus in the Champions League semi-final. In the return leg United found themselves 3-1 down on aggregate at the San Siro. Driven by an inspired Roy Keane, they fought back to take a place in the final.

The drama continued to the last day of the season when United came back to secure the win they needed at Tottenham and take the title. In comparison, the FA Cup Final against Newcastle was uneventful, with Sheringham's early goal settling nerves and Scholes's second-half strike bringing the Cup back to Old Trafford.

And so to Barcelona for a night no fan will ever forget as United, missing Keane and Scholes, incredibly snatched victory from the jaws of defeat at the hands of Bayern Munich. They were the first team ever to win the Premier League, FA Cup and Champions League Treble.

TOP 10 GREATEST GAMES OF ALL TIME

Manchester United have been involved in so many great performances through the years and inevitably it's hard to select a top ten. However, here are some landmark matches and other games which celebrate the brilliant individual displays, magnificent team efforts and momentous achievements that have helped build the club's peerless reputation. Whether you were there in person, watched on TV or online, or have read about them in old newspaper reports, all these games have thrilled and excited fans.

▶ Best and Busby with the European Cup, 1968 and Solskjaer celebrates scoring the second goal during the Champions League Final, 1999

10

TOP 10 GREATEST GAMES OF ALL TIME

TEN MEN HAD SALVAGED A DRAW

Competition: League Division One
Teams: Liverpool vs Manchester United
Date: 4 April 1988
Venue: Anfield, Liverpool
Final score: Liverpool 3-3 Manchester United

▲ Alex Ferguson watches his team from the touchline against Liverpool at Anfield, 4 April 1988

It was Alex Ferguson's first full season in charge at Old Trafford, but there was still work to do. United were in second place in the league when they travelled to Anfield, but the hosts were in their pomp. Liverpool were 11 points clear at the top with two games in hand and the title was all but theirs.

It might have been a sunny Bank Holiday Monday, but no game between these teams was ever going to be an exhibition match. As the *Times*' match report from Martin Searby highlighted, it would have been difficult to conceive of a game more filled with passion, pace, skill and commitment than that provided by the two sides at the top of the First Division.

In just the third minute United were a goal to the good. Excellent work from Brian McClair and Peter Davenport had set up Bryan Robson for a tap-in. Despite tackles flying in, both sides played some flowing football and one such move enabled Peter Beardsley to equalise. This Liverpool side were hard to suppress and before the break the pressure told as Gillespie's header put them in front.

Immediately after the break, things got worse for United as Steve McMahon fired a stunning shot past keeper Chris Turner to make it 3-1. It was a fair reflection of the control Liverpool had shown, but United never gave up. They threw themselves into challenges and introduced Norman Whiteside into the fray. Then Colin Gibson collected a second yellow and received his marching orders. They had ten men, were two goals down and facing the best team in the country. With 30 minutes still to play, things looked grim.

Just six minutes later, though, United had hope. A speculative 25-metre shot from Bryan Robson took a wicked deflection that wrong-footed Liverpool keeper Bruce Grobbelaar and spun into the net. The ten men fought on. After 78 minutes, Davenport turned neatly and chipped a ball through the square Liverpool defence. Gordon Strachan ran onto it, but rather than take on Grobelaar paused and coolly stroked the ball home. It was 3-3. Incredibly, the ten men had salvaged a draw. The Kop were briefly silenced then incensed as Strachan grinned and puffed on an imaginary cigar. It was an image United fans would cherish for many years.

ITALIAN TEENAGER SAVED THE SEASON

Competition: Premier League
Teams: Manchester United vs Aston Villa
Date: 5 April 2009
Venue: Old Trafford, Manchester
Final score: Manchester United 3-2 Aston Villa

▲ Federico Macheda of Manchester United celebrates scoring their third goal against Aston Villa at Old Trafford, 5 April 2009

For the first time since 2005 Manchester United had lost two consecutive league games, including an embarrassing 4-1 thrashing by Liverpool at Old Trafford. They had squandered a ten-point lead at the top of the table and now Liverpool, who had played the day before, had gone top.

With six first-choice players missing, including Rio Ferdinand, Nemanja Vidić and Wayne Rooney, United looked vulnerable. Visitors Villa duly caused problems on the counter-attack, so it came as a surprise when United took the lead. With an indirect free-kick 10 metres from goal, Giggs rolled the ball to Ronaldo, who curled home from a wide angle. The home side took control, but were never comfortable against Villa's pacey counter-attacks and eventually one such move resulted in Carew heading the equaliser.

Villa slowly built up a head of steam in the second half. On 58 minutes the slackness that had characterised United's play led to Gabriel Agbonlahor beating Van der Sar to a cross and giving Villa the lead. As United fans wondered just how their team could dig themselves out of this hole, Ferguson took a massive gamble. He brought on 17-year-old Italian Federico Macheda for his debut. The youngster's zip energised an up-until-now turgid United. He had a good shout for a penalty and made inroads on the left wing, but time was running out.

It took a stroke of brilliance to level the game. With just ten minutes left a neat interchange of passing between Giggs and Carrick on the edge of the box led to the ball being switched across to Ronaldo. He took a touch before squeezing a deadly accurate shot between Villa keeper Brad Friedel's left hand and the post. The game was tantalisingly balanced: United had the momentum, but Villa kept counter-attacking.

As desperate defending and fabulous saves kept the scores level, it looked like United's season was falling apart. Then, in injury time, Macheda received the ball with his back to goal. After a back-heel flick and a delicious turn, he leant back and curled a shot into the far corner of the net for the winner. United would not lose another game and finished four points clear on top, but no one will ever forget the day the Italian teenager saved the season.

THE END OF THE TROPHY FAMINE

Competition: FA Cup Final
Teams: Manchester United vs Liverpool
Date: 21 May 1977
Venue: Wembley Stadium, London
Final score: Manchester United 2-1 Liverpool

It was Tommy Docherty's crowning moment as a Manchester United manager, a marker that United were back at the top end of English football and the greatest five minutes of FA Cup Final football — and for those who enjoy a little schadenfreude, it sank high-flying rivals Liverpool.

Having lost the previous year's final to second division Southampton, it had now been nine years since United had won any major silverware. Docherty had promised United's fans that his side would be back next year to win the Cup. Sure enough they made the final, but faced Liverpool, league champions and European Cup finalists.

United gained the first advantage, winning the toss to wear their traditional red shirts, but when the game got underway it was clear the tension and the stifling heat had sucked the energy from both teams. For all of United's exciting, attacking reputation and Liverpool's class, the first half was a cagey affair with little goalmouth action.

The match exploded into life shortly after the break in what became known as the "Five Minute Final". Sammy McIlroy intercepted a Keegan header in midfield, directing it forwards. The ball bounced high on the hard surface and Jimmy Greenhoff flicked it on again for Stuart Pearson, who charged into the area and beat Ray Clemence with a fierce shot to the near post. Despite the noise generated by the United fans, Liverpool came straight back at them, equalising two minutes later with a terrific spin and shot by Jimmy Case.

The game and the stadium had come to life. United were on the front foot hustling and moving forward at every opportunity. It paid dividends almost immediately. Lou Macari flicked on a long ball and Jimmy Greenhoff put Liverpool defender Tommy Smith under pressure in the area. As the ball fell loose, Macari arrived to hit a hopeful shot. It would have sailed high and wide had it not deflected off Greenhoff's chest and looped over the stranded Clemence. It was the flukiest goal ever, but that didn't bother the ecstatic United fans.

United held firm for the rest of the game and celebrated a famous victory. They had ended the trophy famine, put paid to Liverpool's Treble hopes and fans were able to dream what this young side might now achieve…

▼ Brian Greenhoff (centre) lifting the FA Cup with his brother Jimmy who scored United's second and winning goal in the final against Liverpool at Wembley

THE NIGHT ROBSON OVERSHADOWED MARADONA

Competition: UEFA Cup-Winners' Cup
Teams: Manchester United vs Barcelona
Date: 21 March 1984
Venue: Old Trafford, Manchester
Final score: Manchester United 3-0 Barcelona

It is widely accepted that the atmosphere on that day in March 1984 was the most electric Old Trafford has ever seen. From the moment the players emerged, the 60,000 fans created a wall of noise. United were 2-0 down from the first leg and facing a gifted Barcelona team that included Diego Maradona and Bernd Schuster. They needed all the help they could get.

Ron Atkinson's side were no pushovers themselves. They were unbeaten in 16 league games and had gone top four days earlier by thrashing Arsenal 4-0. The manager kept the same team with young defender Graeme Hogg deputising for the injured Gordon McQueen and Bryan Robson spearheading a midfield containing Remi Moses, Ray Wilkins and Norman Whiteside.

United started on the front foot and an early lobbed shot from Whiteside hit the bar. Then, on 23 minutes, a Wilkins cross was flicked on by the young Northern Irishman and Robson's tumbling far-post header fell into an empty net. The fans became even more passionate and Barcelona were clearly rattled.

The visitors were still ahead on aggregate at half-time, but not for much longer. Just five minutes of the second half had elapsed when Arnold Mühren's low cross picked out Wilkins in the box. His clipped first-time shot was only parried by the keeper and it was Robson again who was on hand to tap in. It was 2-0 on the night and United were level.

Another 82 seconds was all it took. Driven on by

▶ Captain Bryan Robson (left) of Manchester United shakes hands with Barcelona captain Diego Maradona before the European Cup-Winners' Cup quarter-final second leg match between Manchester United and Barcelona held on 21 March 1984 at Old Trafford

the Old Trafford roar, United attacked again. Robson sprayed a cross-field ball down to the touchline, from where Arthur Albiston sent in a deep cross. Whiteside rose at the far post, nodding the ball across the goal to an unmarked Frank Stapleton who blasted it home.

There was still 30 minutes left. A Moses effort and a Robson flying header nearly made it four, but it was tense. An equaliser would see Barcelona through on away goals and the visitors had their chances: a penalty appeal, some good saves by Gary Bailey and a Schuster shot just went wide. It seemed the final whistle would never come, but when it did fans streamed onto the pitch and carried their Captain Marvel shoulder high. It would be remembered as the night Old Trafford rocked and Bryan Robson overshadowed the great Maradona.

A DEFEAT, BUT A GLORIOUS DEFEAT

Competition: Champions League quarter-final
Teams: Manchester United vs Real Madrid
Date: 23 April 2003
Venue: Old Trafford, Manchester
Final score: Manchester United 4-3 Real Madrid

▲ David Beckham scores a sublime free kick over the Real Madrid wall and past the helpless Casillas

Not every great game results in victory. This thriller might have seen United eliminated from the Champions League, but the Old Trafford crowd witnessed a pulsating battle between two brilliant sides and a virtuoso performance from one of the game's greats.

Real Madrid's Galacticos had stormed away in the first leg. A goal from Luis Figo and two from Raul had threatened a rout, before Ruud van Nistelrooy's strike gave some hope for the return at Old Trafford. Overturning a 3-1 reverse from the first leg was still a mighty challenge. A goal for the visitors would make it almost impossible — and this was a side that featured three Ballon d'Or winners in Figo, Zidane and Ronaldo.

After only 12 minutes those fears were realised when a flowing move ended with Ronaldo powering in a shot from the edge of the area. United were stunned. They worked hard to get a foothold in the game, creating half-chances but always vulnerable to the attacking power of the visitors. Three minutes before the break, Solskjær's brave work resulted in Van Nistelrooy bundling the ball into an open goal. It was a slim lifeline, but the Old Trafford faithful gratefully grabbed it.

Whatever they expected, it wasn't what happened next. Just after the break — in the space of eight minutes — a superb interchange of passes from Zidane and Roberto Carlos put Ronaldo through for his second goal, United grabbed one back when Juan Sebastián Verón's shot was deflected in, but Ronaldo was in sparkling form and sent a stunning 25-metre drive past Fabien Barthez for his hat-trick. At 3-2 surely it was over?

The Brazilian was soon substituted, leaving the field to a sporting and appreciative standing ovation from the Old Trafford crowd, but it was another substitution that gave the game another twist. David Beckham, who had been controversially left out of the team, replaced Verón. He soon sent one of his superb free kicks past Casillas in the Madrid goal and then scrambled a loose ball over the line to put United ahead on the night. In what would be his final European minutes for the club, Beckham pushed in vain for another. Ultimately, it was a defeat, but a glorious defeat in which United had shown a heroic refusal to collapse against an all-star team at their very best.

ROMA SHELL-SHOCKED BY A RAMPANT UNITED

Competition: Champions League quarter-final
Teams: Manchester United vs Roma
Date: 10 April 2007
Venue: Old Trafford, Manchester
Final score: Manchester United 7-1 Roma

Alex Ferguson had predicted that if the team scored, which he thought they would, they would pull this one off — and he turned out to be quite the clairvoyant. His side did just that and much, much more in a game he would later describe as one of the defining performances in the history of the club and the finest European display Old Trafford had ever witnessed.

United had lost 2-1 in the first leg in Rome, but that Wayne Rooney away goal gave them a fair chance of progressing in the second leg. However, the home side were missing Paul Scholes after his red card in Rome and fielded a central midfield of Michael Carrick and Darren Fletcher. Up front Wayne Rooney was partnered by Alan Smith, who had recently returned to action after a long absence.

Roma hero Francesco Totti's fizzing shot in the early minutes could have foretold a difficult evening for the hosts. In fact, it did anything but. United immediately got into their stride with crisp passing and players finding space with ease. Over eight first-half minutes, they shocked the Italian giants and established a stranglehold on the tie.

First to net was Carrick. On 11 minutes, Cristiano Ronaldo made inroads into the opponents' half before teeing up the midfielder, who elegantly clipped the ball into the roof of the net from 20 metres. Six minutes later, Giggs's cross-field pass bounced nicely into the path of Smith, who smashed a half volley — his first goal for United since November 2005. When Rooney tucked

▲ Alan Smith of Manchester United celebrates scoring their second goal with Darren Fletcher and Wayne Rooney

away a third from Giggs's cross on 19 minutes, fans were in dreamland.

Roma were shell-shocked. They pushed forward and tried to find a way back, but just left more space for a rampant United, who attacked with speed and penetration. Ronaldo's low drive inside the right post — his first European goal — just before half-time ended the match as a competition. The rest was exhibition stuff: sliding in at the far post, Ronaldo made it five; another delicious long-distance strike by Carrick into the top corner was the sixth; and despite Daniele De Rossi's superb volley giving the Italian's a slither of consolation, when Evra's bobbling shot crept in, it proved that this was United's night. It was a fantastic display from every single player. Alex Ferguson couldn't hide his glee and who could blame him.

SOMETHING SPECIAL TO REMEMBER THEM BY

Competition: League Division One
Teams: Arsenal vs Manchester United
Date: 1 February 1958
Venue: Highbury, London
Final score: Arsenal 4-5 Manchester United

There were 63,000 spectators packed into Highbury on a February afternoon, drawn by an exciting young United team described that day in the Daily Express as near to being the best soccer machine ever created. Manchester United, having won the league in the two previous seasons, were not only chasing a third, but possibly a historic Treble. They were that good.

This game would be the last time anyone saw the great Busby Babes team play on English soil. Within five days, after a draw in Belgrade, five of the team who featured at the Arsenal Stadium that day would be dead and the heart ripped out of a club on the verge of greatness.

However, this match was every bit good enough to be remembered in its own right. Home or away, United attacked with speed and passed with purpose and this was no exception. The first half showed the young side in their pomp as Duncan Edwards's shot from the edge of the area put them one up after 11 minutes. On the half-hour, after a 70-metre sprint from Scanlon, the ball was crossed to Bobby Charlton who smashed it home. United were in total command with two Charlton efforts cleared off the line before Tommy Taylor swept in a third from Kenny Morgans's pass. It was 3-0 at half-time and the game looked done and dusted.

Arsenal had other ideas, though. They came out for the second half and in the space of 150 seconds had, amazingly, levelled the tie through David Herd (who would join United in 1961) and two from Jimmy Bloomfield. The volume of the Highbury faithful went sky high as a famous victory suddenly looked possible, but it was United who were galvanised.

It was as if they shifted gear and started playing again, their intricate passing game coming back to the fore. Charlton fed Albert Scanlon who delivered a cross to Dennis Viollet who headed United back into the lead. Then neat play from Eddie Colman and Morgans set up Taylor to net from a tight angle. Now it was 5-3 and once again United were coasting. There was still time for Arsenal to pull one back, but although no one knew it, this Manchester United team had truly delivered something special to remember them by.

▼ Manchester United players Tommy Taylor, left, and Ken Morgans, line up before playing Arsenal at their Highbury Stadium, 1 February 1958. This was Taylor's last match, he died in the plane crash that killed eight of the Busby Babes team in Munich less than a week later

GIGGS' NEVER-TO-BE-FORGOTTEN MAGIC MOMENT

Competition: FA Cup semi-final replay
Teams: Manchester United vs Arsenal
Date: 14 April 1999
Venue: Villa Park, Birmingham
Final score: Manchester United 2-1 Arsenal

It was one of the best ties in the history of the FA Cup. It had everything. Two teams close to the peak of their powers, simmering rivalry that constantly threatened to boil over, a sending off, great goals and saves, and consequences that might well have changed the course of English football.

A few days earlier the first game, also at Villa Park in Birmingham, had ended in a 0-0 draw. What it had shown was that there was little to separate the two best teams in the country: Arsenal, who were eyeing a successive Double, and United who were chasing a possible Treble. It was the unstoppable, swaggering, attacking force of United against the immovable, resolute Gunners' defence and something had to give.

With just over a quarter of an hour gone, United finally broke through. David Beckham picked up a loose ball and charged into the Arsenal half. Exchanging passes with Teddy Sheringham, he found himself in space and, from 22 metres, curled a magnificent virtual free-kick past the sprawling David Seaman in the Arsenal goal.

As an enthralling game went into the second half, United had the upper hand with Ole Gunnar Solskjær and Jesper Blomqvist both going close to adding a second. The Gunners were too good to roll over, though. Ryan Giggs and Marc Overmars came on as substitutes, and the game went up another gear. Dennis Bergkamp's superb turn and shot from distance was deflected past Peter Schmeichel and the game was level.

▲ Ryan Giggs celebrates after dancing through the Arsenal defence and scoring a magnificent winner

Now Arsenal pushed for the winner. In the heated aftermath of a disallowed goal, Roy Keane received his marching orders and then in injury time the Londoners were awarded a penalty. United's hopes were hanging by a thread. Bergkamp struck it to Peter Schmeichel's left, but the keeper dived low and parried it away.

A man to the good, Arsenal had the upper hand as the game went into extra-time. Then, with just ten minutes remaining, Ryan Giggs intercepted a misplaced pass from a tired Patrick Vieira. He drove into Arsenal's half, dribbled through three defenders and burst past two more before shooting into the roof of the net. One never-to-be-forgotten magic moment had not only settled the tie, but knocked the stuffing out of their rivals and given United the belief and momentum to go on and win the Treble.

THE PRIZE THAT ENGLISH FOOTBALL HAD DREAMED OF

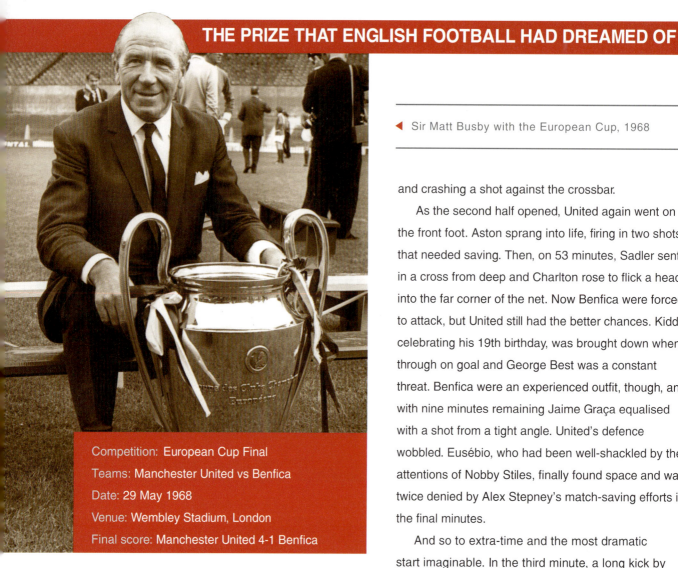

◀ Sir Matt Busby with the European Cup, 1968

Competition: European Cup Final
Teams: Manchester United vs Benfica
Date: 29 May 1968
Venue: Wembley Stadium, London
Final score: Manchester United 4-1 Benfica

The European Cup. It was the prize that English football had dreamed of, but it was a tough challenge. Despite playing the final on home soil at Wembley, United had to overcome five-times finalists Benfica, who boasted the great Eusébio, while missing their own star Denis Law.

Playing in an unfamiliar all-blue kit, United made the running from the start with their opponents happy to defend and resort to rough tackling. Nevertheless, United went close on several occasions, with John Aston, Bobby Charlton, Brian Kidd and David Sadler all linking up to good effect. Not that Benfica were impotent, with Eusébio taking two dangerous free-kicks and crashing a shot against the crossbar.

As the second half opened, United again went on the front foot. Aston sprang into life, firing in two shots that needed saving. Then, on 53 minutes, Sadler sent in a cross from deep and Charlton rose to flick a header into the far corner of the net. Now Benfica were forced to attack, but United still had the better chances. Kidd, celebrating his 19th birthday, was brought down when through on goal and George Best was a constant threat. Benfica were an experienced outfit, though, and with nine minutes remaining Jaime Graça equalised with a shot from a tight angle. United's defence wobbled. Eusébio, who had been well-shackled by the attentions of Nobby Stiles, finally found space and was twice denied by Alex Stepney's match-saving efforts in the final minutes.

And so to extra-time and the most dramatic start imaginable. In the third minute, a long kick by Stepney was headed on by Kidd to Best. The Belfast Boy brilliantly beat the defender, rounded the keeper and tapped the ball into an undefended goal. Two minutes later, Sadler's header from a corner was diverted by Kidd. The keeper could only parry it out and the birthday boy made no mistake with his second attempt. Benfica were shell-shocked and United kept coming; hitting the crossbar, before Charlton made it 4-1 by clipping in a low cross after brilliant work from man-of-the-match Aston.

Fittingly it was Bobby Charlton, a survivor of Munich, who lifted the Cup. It was a trophy the players had promised to win for Matt Busby, who had suffered so much and worked so hard for this great club.

CUE THE TREBLE MAYHEM

Competition: Champions League Final
Teams: Manchester United vs Bayern Munich
Date: 26 May 1999
Venue: Old Trafford, Manchester
Final score: Nou Camp, Barcelona

In a season in which United had staged a number of remarkable comebacks, they saved the best for last. Having already secured the Premier League title and the FA Cup, the Champions League was the last part of the Treble. In their way stood the might Bayern Munich, newly crowned Bundesliga champions.

Without both Roy Keane and Paul Scholes, who were missing through suspension, Alex Ferguson plumped for David Beckham to partner Nicky Butt in the centre of midfield with Ryan Giggs and Jesper Blomqvist on the flanks, and he gave Peter Schmeichel the captain's armband in his final Manchester United appearance.

Even ardent United fans would agree that Bayern were the better team for most of the match at Barcelona's Nou Camp. After Mario Basler's ninth-minute low free kick deceived Peter Schmeichel to give the German team an early lead, Manchester United struggled to make an impact. They had plenty of possession, but Bayern held firm and often looked the more dangerous team, Blomqvist having United's best chance when he threw himself at a Giggs cross.

As the clock ran down Alex Ferguson introduced Teddy Sheringham and then Ole Gunnar Solskjær. However, Bayern's substitute Mehmet Scholl seemed more effective, setting up a close Stefan Effenburg effort and hitting the post himself. With just a single goal lead, the game was still tight. Solskjær's header needed a good response from Oliver Kahn in the Bayern goal and an audacious overhead kick by Carsten Jancker rebounded

▲ Ole Gunnar Solskjaer celebrates scoring the second goal during the Champions League Final against Bayern Munich in the Nou Camp, 26 May 1999

off the United crossbar. With just five minutes left the red shirts flooded forward looking for a chance. They found some hope in Sheringham's volley and another header from Solskjær's, but Kahn was equal to them.

Three minutes was added on and 30 seconds of that had elapsed when United won a corner. Schmeichel joined the mêlée in the area as Beckham put in a dangerous cross. Bayern scrambled the ball clear and it fell to Giggs, whose volley was diverted into the net by Sheringham. They had rescued the game at the death and the Munich team were devastated.

United came again from the kick-off. Less than 30 seconds after the equaliser they won another corner. This time Schmeichel cautiously stayed back. Beckham's cross took a lower trajectory, but found Sheringham, whose flick was turned by Solskjær's outstretched foot. Cue mayhem and Schmeichel cartwheeling in his goalmouth. The Treble had been won — and in the most amazing way possible.